East Meadow Public Library

East Meadow, New York

516-794-2570

www.eastmeadow.info

# <u>Deer Hunting 101</u>

## *The Beginner's Guide to Deer Hunting*

author:
**David B. Pruet**

*As the deer pants for streams of water,
so my soul pants for you, O God.
Psalm 42:1*

to order this book go to
*www.booksbydave.com*

Bloomington, IN                    Milton Keynes, UK

*AuthorHouse™*
*1663 Liberty Drive, Suite 200*
*Bloomington, IN 47403*
*www.authorhouse.com*
*Phone: 1-800-839-8640*

*AuthorHouse™ UK Ltd.*
*500 Avebury Boulevard*
*Central Milton Keynes, MK9 2BE*
*www.authorhouse.co.uk*
*Phone: 08001974150*

*First published by AuthorHouse   6/14/2006*

*ISBN: 1-4259-3818-3 (sc)*

*Printed in the United States of America
Bloomington, Indiana*

*This book is printed on acid-free paper.*

*Permission requests and further contact to this author may be addressed
at:  www.booksbydave.com*
*Library of Congress Control Number: 2006904367*
*The author is also available for appearances, interviews, and book
signings per your request. Please contact him to discuss booking these
types of events or to set up an appearance to speak on behalf of hunting
or one of his other special interest topics.*

# CONTENTS

# DEDICATION

I dedicate this book to my wife, Donna, who I know sits at home many days and nights each year worrying about the personal welfare of her selfish husband (we get that way at deer season) while I foolishly go off into the woods hunting something much smarter than I am.

I know she sits there wondering if I've made it to my hunting destination to begin with; contemplating if I've been shot at by another moron hunter who doesn't know the foggiest about hunting safety; or even worried that I've fallen asleep in my tree stand and once again, left myself suspended 20-30 feet above ground level looking like a nine-legged cat trying to scratch and claw my way back up into the very stand I just fell out of. (I hate it when that kind of stuff happens – but it does!)

So, to my lovely bride – I say *"thank you"* for letting me do what I love to do year in and year out. Your love, patience, and understanding are not overlooked and are greatly appreciated. *"I love you babe."*

# FOREWORD

## By: Hunter/Author/Friend
## Mark Thomas

Where was this book in the 70's?! Long before the infamous "...for Dummies" string of books came along; guys like me had precious little basic rudimentary information. I remember spending hours hacking away at my first personal computer calling it everything from silicon-slop to over-priced-boat-anchor. It seemed nothing ever went as expected. The owner's manual was little or no help because it was written by a computer genius with the English writing skills of a foreign exchange student. Whitetail hunting was no different. I, and my whitetail-hunting wannabe brethren, were relegated to trial-and-error, folklore, and advertising misinformation.

_No longer_. Now there's a book for the beginning whitetail hunter that's loaded with basic need-to-know information. Dave could have easily titled this book "Everything You Always Wanted To Know About Hunting Whitetails, but were afraid to ask". The beginning hunter, or seriously interested, now have a resource to get them started. A primer if you will, that will eliminate the pain of trial-and-error and cut through the fog of hunting rhetoric to provide easy step-by-step instruction. Dave takes the reader by the hand and leads him to the promised land of successful whitetail hunting starting at ground zero.

What weapon should I use? What about camo? Am I required to take a test of some sort? How important is scent-proof clothing? Where should I hunt? What do I do after the harvest? How much money is this going to cost? Is hunting whitetail deer for me? These questions and many, many, more run through the minds of beginners every day. Not everyone has a friend to take them under their wing. Not everyone had a mom or dad teach them the hunting lifestyle. Dave is that friend or uncle that you never had. In this book, Dave answers a good number of these questions utilizing an easy-to-follow systematic approach.

Successful hunters all have one thing in common – they are constantly learning about their quarry. I believe experienced hunters will appreciate the information in this book, as well as the beginner and the sports-enthusiast wondering if whitetail hunting is for him or her. Some will learn a great deal, and everyone will learn something – *guaranteed*!

I recently read a story about a fellow who attempted to check an adolescent elk into a <u>*deer*</u> check-in station in the Midwest where elk are making an incredible comeback. My immediate reaction was, "This guy should have read Dave's book". That mistake cost one young man a great deal of money, not to mention a huge embarrassment. That's an extreme case, but many of us make the same mistakes over and over before finally learning what we're doing wrong. *Not so any more*!

Dave and I have been friends for a number of years and I can tell you, he knows his whitetail. He can find them, hunt them, butcher them, cook them and prepare them to hang on the wall. Skim the following pages and see if there isn't something that catches *your* eye. Believe me; <u>you need this book in your library</u>!

Note From The Author:

Be sure to check out Mark's book too -
**"Where Adventure Meets Discovery"**
*-one man's hunting and outdoor odyssey-*
Find it at <u>www.authorhouse.com</u>

# ABOUT THE AUTHOR

 Author Dave Pruet is a man that has hunted the majority of his life beginning with simple, small game species which eventually turned into the love that he now shares with so many around the world - North American Big Game Hunting. His Preference? The great *Whitetail Deer*.

Dave has harvested many different species of game but his true love is pursuing this one species in particular. He works very hard year round talking with game officials and hunting buddies; researching past and present wildlife data; scouting potential hunting areas; even tracking this great animal through its own back yard. All of this has developed into a great sense of respect for the integrity and instinctive nature that this magnificent animal exemplifies. Dave never underestimates the keen senses of the most-sought-after big game species in the world. These, among others, are but a few reasons why so many have come to both love and hate this elusive animal with a passion. If you think hunting whitetail deer is easy, it's not, so don't let anyone tell you that it is.

Few hunters end their hunting season with a deer to fill their freezers, and even fewer have the opportunity to down one that is worthy of dropping off at the local taxidermist. Dave has processed many in both of these manners and now hunts one specific deer at a time. Using only bow and arrow, ("gun just seems too unfair," he claims), he gathers all of his preseason data and mentally takes it with him into the field in hopes of luring that one particular deer he has been pursuing into his shooting range. This is where his training and expertise will pay off – this is what makes him a true 'trophy hunter' - this is what makes him the proficient and admirable hunter he is today.

Dave has a wall full of trophy bucks, many he has mounted himself as he is both State and Federally licensed in the art of Taxidermy. He even has a couple that have made the record books, but he is always searching for that one buck that will be the 'Buck of a Lifetime'. At the time of the writing of this book, Dave is currently on his 3rd season of hunting one buck in particular, and although the buck has presented himself a couple of times, Dave has chosen *not* to take the shot as he is also a firm believer in the theory of 'ethical hunting'. He does not want to take the chance of just injuring a deer. Besides, this would only lead to it running off with little or no chance of an immediate recovery and its demise would ultimately be due to a poor choice or an improperly-placed shot on his behalf. Dave believes that this is what all hunters should believe, for injuring a deer and not finding it due to an urgent desire to just shoot is not only a waste of good meat for the dinner table, but it is an inhumane act at best.

Remember this – '**Don't shoot until you are sure it will be a good, clean, ethical kill**'. You will be a better hunter for it in the long run and most of all, you will thank yourself when it is all said and over with. There is nothing worse than knowing that an animal is out there 'somewhere' suffering because of your greed.

**a portion of the author's "Game Room"**

Another attribute of the author is if you ask him for help in understanding a hunter's insight, he is eager to share what he has learned over the years. If you ask Dave to help you sight in your gun or your bow, he is there for you on that also. You see, Dave is not only a whitetail deer hunter, but Dave is a Christian man who believes in helping his fellow brother or sister in whatever capacity he can. It is his intent, with this book, to help others that can not get to him for his advice; to be able to benefit from his years of experience so that they too may enjoy this outdoors sport he enjoys so much. Dave wants to share, if you want to learn.

Dave is also a professional musician and use to tour on the country music circuit out of Nashville, Tennessee. He also teaches a Christian Outdoorsman's class at his church of 3000 strong appropriately named, "*The Master's Lodge*," and he is a husband, father, son, brother, and good friend to many.

If you ask Dave what he loves to do with his idle time, his first answer may be that he has no idle time. But if you ask him what he would rather do more than anything else, (other than watch his 17 year old daughter Kayla, *dance beautifully*;

or his 15 year old son Kevin, *play some serious soccer*) he would probably say that he would want to "hunt." Dave loves to hunt, but more importantly, he loves '*the hunt*'. It isn't so much about the kill as it is the preparation; the pursuit; and most of all, the seclusion of the woods. If a 'Buck of a Lifetime' just happens to wander into his shooting lane during this time...well, that would be considered a 'bonus for the day' and you can rest assured he would not pass up the opportunity to take the animal down and fill his tag for that season. You see, deer hunting isn't a pastime for Dave, just as it isn't for many serious hunters – it is a PASSION. And with this passion comes a love for the outdoors arena that has been placed within our reach by the greatest Creator of them all. It is here, that Dave feels closer to God than anywhere else on this earth, and he invites you to take the challenge of hanging from a tree just like He hung from one for you. (*see the poem at the end of this book*).

**secluded drive back to author's house**

Dave has found a new passion to go along with his hunting - writing about his endeavors in the woods. Whether it is by the crystal clear streambeds; or on top of snow-covered ridges; or even in the heated valleys of livestock pastures, Dave believes that the key to keeping the hunting interest at its peak is to share what you know with those that are longing for the same gratification and challenge that he himself has discovered, especially with your kids. *"Like everything else in life, our kids are the future of this sport and if we don't teach them, then this incredible sport will eventually die out."*

**author with his son on his *first* deer hunt**

This book is the beginning of a series of self-help hunting books that Dave is currently completing. Be sure to look for others to fill your 'library of knowledge'. You will find these at his site: ***www.booksbydave.com***.

# INTRODUCTION

So, you're interested in hunting? Great!

Hunting is a natural activity for humans as our ancestors were hunters for thousands of years before and even after people learned to grow crops and raise animals for their own food source. Even though food for most people comes from big farms today, many of us still enjoy hunting simply because our ancestors did it, and we seem to relish the fact that we are fulfilling a cycle of our own ancestry by doing what our ancestors did. Whether it is for necessity or for sport, regardless of the reason, we still choose to *hunt*!

At the same time, many individuals simply have an interest in either becoming a deer hunter themselves or know someone who is currently a deer hunter and they just want to learn more about this sport that their friend or loved one enjoys so much. These individuals, by instinctive nature, don't really want to stand out and thus are leery to ask about the details of this sport itself for fear of embarrassment of 'not knowing' what they are talking about. I'm here to tell you, there is nothing to be embarrassed about, but I do understand the reservations that some people may feel – a feeling of inferiority or that of being different. Therefore, I have taken the time to write this book for those of you who have a desire to better understand the nature of the deer hunter themselves, and explain what this sport is all about.

This book, written from a hunter's point of view (my own), has been laid out for you to understand _only the basics_ of deer hunting. I have included some 'Fast Facts' for you to be able to quickly skim through each area of interest should time be of the essence. There are also 'quick-reference' notes that are listed in **Bold Font** and should be very easy to locate as well.

If there is something that you don't understand, or information you can not find in this particular book once you have finished reading it, I encourage you to pursue your research with other publications, including those that I am currently publishing, to help advance your knowledge in this area. You can watch for my next published books to come out on my website: _www.booksbydave.com_.

But, in regards to this book you are holding in your hands right now, I have simply made an attempt to educate the non-hunter in the very basics of this outdoors sport to give them a place to begin. A place to finally understand the phenomenon behind this popular sport.

Let's begin by defining that there are many different species of deer around the world (blacktail deer, whitetail deer, mule deer, fallow deer, axis deer, etc.) but I am going to concentrate this book on the most common of all these species – the infamous North American Whitetail Deer.

I am going to focus the geographical location around the Midwest region of the United States as well as reference the hunter as being a 'male' even though I realize there are many hunters who are female. I do this only because I get tired of writing he/she or him/her throughout the book, so please don't contact me telling me I'm being discriminatory to either sex – that's not my intention at all.

Although I am providing you with a unique tool for preparing to hunt deer, you will be required to (and should) expand your research into your own geographical area in order to better ascertain the true understanding of both the gaming laws and the character traits of the whitetail deer in your area as they do differ.

# Preface

# KNOW YOUR GAME

## *What is a deer?*

One of the first things that we need to cover in this book is identifying the animal in which we intend to hunt. Without this tidbit of information, a soon-to-be deer hunter might one day come home with an animal that he *thought* was a deer, when in all actuality, it was not. This would not be good nor would it be in the best interest of the hunter – neither legally nor ethically. Here, let me give you an example of what I am talking about – and remember - this is a *true* story:

PERSONAL STORY

*It was the early winter season of 1988 and I had just returned from the edge of a cornfield that I had been successful at harvesting deer from in seasons past, but unfortunately, this day had not produced that same opportunity. On the way home I thought that I would stop off at my favorite hunting store which was also a deer 'check-in' station (a place you must take the deer after you kill it) to see if anyone else had been granted a successful day in the woods since my day had come to an end with a tag unfulfilled (a 'tag' is a part of the hunting license that you put on the deer after you kill it identifying the details of the kill).*

*We were all sitting around the pot-belly stove (a pot-belly stove is...never mind) telling stories of the 'big boy in the woods' when the front door of the shop flew open and in came a slender man dressed all in hunter's orange (hunter's orange is a bright orange color you wear so other hunters can identify you from an animal in the woods and don't shoot you). I mean, this guy was dressed in orange from head to toe, so much that he looked like a walking highway cone! The look on his face told the story – he had been successful – but at what? As he approached us he was smiling from ear-to-ear and he boldly stated that he had just killed his first deer! We all sort of looked at each other like, "this guy killed a deer? You have GOT to be kidding me. He looks more like he should be teaching a class at the local college or fixing a computer or something." But we all took his word for it and got up from our warm seats to mosey out the door to see just how big this 'brute' was that he claimed to have killed.*

*As we walked out the front door, snow flying and wind blowing, we looked around for his truck to see which way to head so we could get a quick look and then get back inside to the warmth of the stove. After all, when you've seen one deer, you've seen them all, right? We were sure "Mr. Peabody" here wasn't going to present us with something we had never seen before – well, we were dead wrong on that one. As we looked over, we noticed the only trucks in the parking lot were ours. As we stood there in dismay, the little guy pushed his way through all of us and headed across the lot to the opposite side from where we were all parked – the side we had affectionately named "The Green Zone" (where the non-hunters usually parked). There was only one vehicle over there and it was a Subaru wagon! I remember thinking to myself, "No way, this guy CAN'T have a deer stuffed into that little thing, and even if he does, he's got to have one heck of a mess that will never clean up!" He rushed over to the car and we followed reluctantly but with curiosity to see just what it was he brought in with such excitement.*

*As we gathered around the back of the car, he opened the hatch and as soon as it reached its full height, Bud, the owner of the shop busted out laughing. I couldn't believe my eyes either. Bud immediately*

3

*said, "Dude, that's a goat!" The little guy frowned at Bud and said, "Hey, now I know it's not the biggest deer in the woods, but it's my first one and I'd like a little respect for that if you don't mind." Bud laughed even louder and said, "No man, I mean it...that's a goat! You've gone and killed some farmer's goat!" With that we all lost it. The man had no idea but he had actually shot a goat (not a deer) – you know, BAAAA! And even more so, he had not only shot a goat, but field dressed the thing (gutted it); drug it through the woods; loaded it in his little Subaru wagon; and then brought it all the way in to the check-in station to have it checked in and recorded. All the time, he had believed that it was actually a deer! We all got a good laugh and Bud told him to take it back to where he killed it and get with the owner before someone called the Possum Cops (Conservation Officers) on him. With his head down and the wind completely out of his sails, the man got back in his little car and drove off. We laughed for years after that every time someone brought it up. Heck, I still laugh about it to this day – now that's hilarious!*

So, with that story in mind, YOUR #1 rule, when hunting *any* type of game should be:

# KNOW WHAT YOU ARE SHOOTING AT!

**THIS IS A DEER**

**THIS IS NOT**

## **Character Traits of the Whitetail Deer**

**A female deer is called a 'doe';
a baby deer is called a 'fawn';
and a male deer is called a 'buck'.**

The buck is the one with antlers (or 'rack' as most deer hunters call them) and is the one that most hunters seek out for their trophy. Female deer and baby deer do not have antlers.

A buck can be up to four feet tall at the top of its back and weigh up to 300 pounds, whereas the female deer is much smaller in size. A doe may have up to three fawns in one litter which will stay with their mother until she eventually drives them off to be on their own just prior to having her next litter.

**Deer are nocturnal animals meaning that they sleep during the day and feed at night** (or when the sun is going down). They travel in small groups which consist of one of two types: Females and Fawns (mothers and babies), or, Batchelor Groups (where 3-5 bucks hang out together). During cooler weather it is not uncommon for deer to form 'herds' where there may be as many as 50-100 deer in one group at the same time. This is true up until the 'rut' (breeding season) which we will discuss in more detail later.

In the winter, the reddish-brown color of the deer changes slightly to a more 'grayish' color in order to allow the deer better camouflage from predators in the wooded areas where they live.

Deer are very responsive to strange smells, sounds, and movement in their areas of comfort. If any of these present something out of the ordinary, they immediately disperse, and if you have ever been in the woods and spooked a deer, you can identify this with the flash of white that you see as they raise their tail, flagging a warning as they flee the area.

Deer are very fast and have been clocked at speeds up to 45 mph. They are extremely agile and can leap as high as 9 feet from a standing position when required to do so.

**author with a trophy Whitetail Buck
taken with a 12ga pump shotgun**

**author with a trophy Whitetail Buck
taken with a compound bow**

# Chapter One

# ABOUT WHITETAIL DEER

## FAST FACT
**Whitetail deer are one of the largest big game animals in the Midwest region. They have a white belly and tail, thus giving them their common name - the 'Whitetail Deer'.**

## Where Do Deer Live?
**Deer are animals that live primarily in wooded areas.** They are sometimes seen out of these 'comfort zones' with sightings in rural areas, fields, by waterways, and even by roadways - ok, show of hands – "How many of you have ever hit a deer with your vehicle?" See what I mean? These sightings are usually due to the fact that they are either searching for food and/or water, or they have been run out of their area by an endangering force such as man or another predatory species like a coyote, a cougar, or other animals that prey on this particular species. Yes, I said a 'cougar'. And please, whatever you do, don't believe the so-called 'experts' that say cougars are only found in certain States – I am here to testify against this theory. Cougars can travel thousands of miles if they need to – I have sighted one

twice right here in the Midwest where I hunt. Not a very comfortable feeling when you think about the time of day you travel when hunting. You begin by walking into the woods in the dark, and then you finish by walking out of the woods in the dark. Me? I just keep walkin' – very quietly I might add, and stay very alert, always.

Of all of the big game animals in North America, the whitetail deer is the most widely distributed and the most plentiful. Its range extends from the southern tip of the North American Continent northward well into the Northern Canadian regions. But again, for purposes of this book, we will concentrate our study on those that are located primarily around my area, in the Midwest region of the United States.

 **White-tailed deer range**

## What Do Deer Eat?

Deer are *herbivores* which means **they eat twigs, green plants, berries, crops, nuts, fruits, and even some types of fungi.** An interesting trait of the deer is that they are just like kids, whereas they will eat their dessert first, and if this source is plentiful, this is all they will eat. Therefore, it is advantageous for the hunter to search for any area which produces an abundance of nuts and fruits. Two of the most common for the Midwest region are oak trees (which produce a large supply of acorns) or during certain parts of the season, persimmon trees (which produce a very sweet fruit that deer go crazy over). Either should produce a high concentrate of deer in these areas.

As far as what do deer drink, of course the only readily available source for them is water. Deer will visit a watering hole 2-3 times a day to get a drink, but if it has been a rainy season, then deer may drink from a small puddle that has formed next to their bedding area, thus, not having to venture far from their 'comfort zone' in order to quench their thirst.

## Where Do Deer Sleep?

Typically, deer look for heavy cover in which to form their bedding areas as this not only provides a wind break for their own comfort, but also provides cover from being in view, for safety reasons. Some of these bedding areas can be found within **heavy brush areas; on the down slope of hillsides; and most preferably, directly under pine trees** (they love the softness of the pine needles and the cover that the large, bushy limbs provide during the snowy months). Deer usually will select a bedding area which faces south in order to be able to absorb the heat from the sun during the peek of the day.

## How Smart Are Deer?
**The whitetail deer is considered to be one of the smartest animals on the face of the earth.** This is mainly attributed to the fact that they have very keen senses and realize that anything that triggers these senses in an unfamiliar fashion means 'danger', and as previously discussed, they possess the ability to out run; out jump; and out smart their enemy.

Let's take a look at these sharp senses:

**A Deer's Sense of 'SIGHT'** – Deer have an incredible amount of 'rods' in their eyes which create the ability to be able to see very clearly at night. This is one of the reasons why they are nocturnal by nature because they can be up and around when most other predators can not. Contrary to earlier beliefs that deer are color blind... this is not true. Deer have the ability to see everything that we as humans see, with the exception of being able to clearly focus on objects that DON'T MOVE. **They pick up movement very well and therefore it is very important to be as still as you can when you hunt.** If a deer sees you and you 'freeze' (don't move), you will typically see the deer change locations to try and locate what they saw before – YOU. They will do this by lowering their head; moving from side to side; changing to another angle in front of or behind you; or even walk toward you and look straight up. Why? They can't focus well on a stationary object and you literally 'disappear' right in front of their eyes. Stay still and wait for them to walk behind a tree or turn their head away – when this happens, raise your weapon and be ready for the shot.

**<u>A Deer's Sense of 'HEARING'</u>** - Next, let's look at the deer's sense of hearing. **Deer can hear at a rate of 10 times that of a human being.** If you have ever seen a guy standing on the sidelines of a football game holding what looks like a small satellite dish, this is a hearing-enhancement device that allows him to be able to pick up sounds from long distances that the normal human ear can not detect. Likewise, the deer's ear is designed like a "mini-dish" and along with their large ears that they 'cup' into a dish-like form, they can pick up sounds that we can not hear. This attribute causes their hearing advantage to be incredibly sensitive. If a deer hears anything that is not conformant to their surroundings...you guessed it – danger, and they are outta there before you are even close enough to know they were there to begin with. So, it is very important to be as quiet as you can from the time you arrive in your vehicle (closing doors silently), until the time that you leave the area (no radio blasting, please!).

**A Deer's Sense of 'SMELL'** - Lastly, the deer's most sensitive of all their senses is their uncanny ability to smell a measly mushroom up to 400 yards away. If you don't listen to anything else I have to say from here on out, <u>listen to this</u>. **If you smell of any foreign odor at all, regardless of if it is a fragrance or some other odor (sweat, gas fumes, cigarette smoke, coffee breath, etc.) that is totally undetectable to the human nose, you can pretty much count on the fact that you are NOT going to see any deer during that**

**day's hunt.** Like I said before, a deer can smell a tiny, little mushroom from 400 yards away - don't think that they can't smell you after you have been sweating while climbing your tree stand, or after you put your coveralls on while standing by your truck's smoking exhaust pipe. I can't stress to you enough how important it is to invest in some cover-up scents; scent-protectant suits and gear; and create a good plan of how not to sweat before, during, and after the hunt, because if you smell at all – they're gone – and again, you won't even know they were there to begin with because they will vacate the area long before you even arrive and their return is doubtful.

## <u>Why Should I Hunt Deer?</u>

Hunting deer is a **sport** of outdoorsmen for the mere fact that it is a huge challenge to take one of these incredible creatures down. It is also a **source of food** for the hunter should he choose to partake of his success. Deer provide a source for some **very healthy meat** because they eat nothing but natural foods and are very healthy animals. But one of the most important reasons to hunt deer is that deer are considered to be **one of the most destructive animals on the face of the earth** costing humans millions of dollars each year in lost crops and automobile-deer accidents.

Many farmers in various states have reported that up to 80% of their crops have been destroyed by large deer herds feeding at night. This crop loss creates an adverse effect on the rising market price of these foods which we shop for in our very own grocery stores.  In the long run, this loss is costing the consumer (you and me) more money each time we go to the store to buy this produce because supply is increasingly less than the abundance of demand for the produce in question.

Although deer are very beautiful and intriguing to watch, they are increasing in numbers at a rate that is becoming more and more difficult to keep up with. Some States provide "special hunts" in order to weed out deer herds in their area to help control the overall population of these animals. It isn't so much to kill off the deer, but too many deer in one area also leads to a limited food supply. This in itself will ultimately result in a slow, agonizing death for the deer that eventually starves to death because it can not find food to survive on through the wintry months.

State and National Conservationists believe that not only are hunters good caretakers of the land, but excellent resources for providing a much-needed wildlife management service throughout the intended area of concentration. Regardless of what anti-hunting; non-hunting; and other animal activist groups may profess, you hunt and you hunt hard. I'm here to tell you it is a good thing to do. You are a vital part of wildlife management that is much appreciated, and more importantly, much needed. Heck, take the whole family hunting and make a day of it! It's been done for years!

# Chapter Two

# PREPARING FOR THE HUNT

**FAST FACT**
**It is very important to be prepared for the hunt prior to venturing into the woods where the whitetail deer live. Know what the deer look like; choose the correct weapon; obtain the proper licenses; wear the appropriate gear; and *practice shooting*. These are the basics for preparing for the hunt.**

However, to start the process, there are many other factors one must consider before going into the woods looking for a monster buck or a tasty doe. Some of these factors have absolutely nothing to do with being in the woods themselves but are vitally important to the overall hunting adventure. Let's take a look at what some of these other factors are:

## What Type Of Weapon Should I Use?
One thing is for sure, when you are planning on going on a hunt, you are going to need something to kill the animal with unless you plan on jumping on its back as it walks by and strangling it to death. Because this kill method is not recommended, **it is important to know**

**what weapon you can afford; feel
comfortable with; and are consistently
accurate with in all situations.**

The majority of hunters utilize the shotgun
for their first weapon of choice. Only those
who are very experienced in the art of
deer hunting choose the bow and arrow
method because this particular weapon
does not have the range that the shotgun
has and therefore requires that the hunter
be savvy enough to lure the deer into
within a 0-40 yard shooting range for
a good, clean shot. Getting a deer this
close to you requires that you had better
understand the senses of the deer and
know all of the 'tricks' required when it
comes to fooling such a smart animal.

Shotguns (usually a 12 gauge), allow for
a special type of *bullet* for hunting deer
that enables the hunter to take a secure
shot up to 80 yards. This special bullet is
called a 'slug' and is a bullet-shaped piece
of lead that has a plastic jacket around it
just like a regular shotgun shell with the
only difference being that you don't have
a spray of little pellets flying at the animal
like you do when you hunt for smaller
game. Rather, you just have the one 'slug'
flying through the air at your intended
target with some extraordinary knock-

down power. You can acquire these at your local sporting goods store or at most department stores.

Be prepared to spend $300 - $1000 for a decent shotgun if you don't have one already, and that is just the gun – you will need more items than that to get started.

**Equipment To Help You Get Started** – If you are going to hunt with a shotgun (as most beginning hunters do), below is a brief list of what you might need to start:

- Shotgun (usually a 12 gauge)
- Ammunition (slugs)
- Hunting license (tags)
- Hunter's Orange safety-wear

That is all that is actually *required* by most State Regulatory Departments (i.e.: DNR – Department of Natural Resources) to go hunting for the whitetail deer, however, I speak from years of experience when I say that you will continually add to your arsenal of both equipment and clothing.

# <u>VARIOUS TYPES OF ARCHERY WEAPONS USED</u>

**Traditional Long Bow**

**Traditional Re-curve Bow**

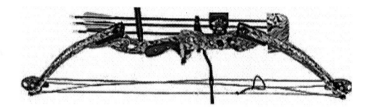

**Modern Compound Bow**

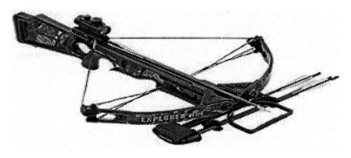

**Modern Cross Bow with a Scope**

# VARIOUS TYPES OF FIREARM WEAPONS USED

**Traditional Flintlock Rifle** (Black Powder)

**Traditional Percussion Cap Rifle** (Black Powder)

**Modern In-Line Muzzleloader with a Scope**

**Standard Pump Shotgun**

**Standard Semi-automatic Shotgun**

**High-powered Rifle with a Scope** (not legal in many States)

**Handgun** (barrel length requirements vary per state)

# <u>What About Camouflage?</u>

There are many reasons for selecting camouflaged clothing based on the individual hunt itself. Some factors to consider when choosing what camouflage pattern might work best for you are:

- Season you plan to hunt
- Terrain you plan to hunt
- Comfort of the clothing
- Does it have scent protection
- Is it quiet when you move around
- Price

We all should realize that we need to  choose a camouflage pattern that is going to match these parameters as best as possible and although mixing and matching various patterns to match a 'specific situation' is not uncommon, most hunters don themselves in the same pattern from head to toe. This isn't a bad thing and is much more practical than having to buy numerous patterns of clothing in order to exactly match the terrain around you. This can be done once you become more serious about the sport and feel it is necessary for you to expand your hunting wardrobe in order for you to increase your chances for success. But for now, my suggestion is to pick one pattern that works as an all-around pattern for your particular area and go with it.

Anything to break up your outline should work and offer some level of 'invisibility' to the deer's sight that you are hunting.

You also have to consider where you plan on hunting from in the woods.

Let's first consider the <u>tree stand hunter</u>: The area he needs to be most concerned about blending into is what is behind him and *above* him since the deer will be looking "up" toward him. In this particular setting, he should match trees, leaves, bark, and of course, the sky.

Another consideration is that of the hunter who does not hunt from a tree stand yet chooses to hunt <u>on the ground</u> - maybe even from a blind as the author does in this picture. He needs to be aware of what is going to be *around* him in order to select the proper camouflage pattern that conforms to those particular surroundings. It could be brush; leaves; trees; bark; corn stalks; weeds; snow; hay; etc.

**Camouflage works because it creates visual confusion in the game that you are hunting. It doesn't make you invisible - far from it - but rather it simply disguises your recognizable form by breaking up your outline.** This visual confusion is created by both the various shapes and colors that make up the pattern you choose. Even for animals without a sharp *color* vision, such as the whitetail deer, the irregular pattern of these different shades and shapes that you are wearing serves to break up your outline which in turn, conceals your 'identity' to the deer. The whole idea of camouflage is to *blend into the environment* so that you can not be recognized as being 'out of place'. Think of someone standing in your living room when you get home – you would definitely notice them right away. Now, think of that same person standing in the corner of your living room with a lampshade on his head – although they will still stand out, you are less likely to recognize them immediately if your mind just sees a 'lamp' as you glance by. Ok, maybe that was a stretch, but you get the idea. You, better than anyone, know where and how you will be hunting so the best thing to do is camo-up (that means buy some camouflage clothing and wear it).

"Ok, how do I choose what is best?" you might ask. Take an overall look at your hunting habitat to determine the predominant color tones and vegetation of that terrain. If you're going to be hunting an area you haven't hunted or even seen before, ask a friend or a guide to help you choose your patterns and color selections.

Also, don't get caught wearing too much 'stuff' because if you wear too much, you will look like a 'blob' in a tree and the deer know there are no squirrels' nests that big in the woods. So, looking at camouflage at a short distance to determine what to buy is not the best test of its effectiveness. Looking at it from a distance where the game sees it tells you much more. There is a natural human tendency to want to see a lot of contrasting colors and shapes or a lot of 'stuff' in the pattern. However, at some distance, a really tight and crowded pattern can once again appear to be a solid color, and this is NOT what you want. This literally destroys the pattern's camouflaging effect and exposes your position immediately. Be simple, be clean.

Ok, now let's look at the most visible areas of your body that a deer will mostly likely detect first. <u>The two most movement-prone areas of your body are your face and your hands</u>. Even when trying to remain completely still, these light, high-contrast areas seem to stand out like a neon light to a whitetail deer. If you remember the last picture that we looked at with the author hunting from a ground blind, you can see his hands and face very clearly. This was presented intentionally for this portion of the book to show how critical it is to wear camouflage on these parts of the body as well.

Complete camouflage should include a face mask or head net, and gloves to be safe. Face masks and gloves are necessities for close-range hunting scenarios such as bow hunting for deer when you have to get the deer in close enough for a shot. A deer will literally watch your eye movement (for real) so either a face mask or head net is a *must*. Remember, they know their own house and they know everything that lives, breathes, and moves in that house too!

The legal requirement that requires a hunter to wear "*Hunter Orange*" (a very bright shade of orange) for most big-game hunting with firearms works against a good camouflage pattern because the orange vest, or whatever is chosen, has to be worn on the outside of the pattern. It is proven that deer can see this highly-reflective color as a 'light blob' which appears in contrast to the drab and darker natural environment it is accustomed to seeing. The best option is to wear a 'camo-orange' pattern that breaks up the orange area the best that it can. However, some States require a solid orange garment with no pattern at all.

In these situations, an orange vest or hat meeting the minimum size requirement, coupled with good camouflage on the more movement-prone head, arms, hands and legs is your best bet.

Check your local regulations carefully as you definitely don't want to be in violation of this law. Some States require a Hunter Orange hat as well but usually the vest is sufficient. Predominantly, orange gloves do not qualify for meeting the minimal square inch requirement in any State, mainly because if you put your hands in your pockets or a hand-warming 'muff', your safety color disappears and that could result in a fatal situation. Believe me, there are hunters out there that have

no concept of safety, and they will only realize their error once the shot has been fired. I, personally, have literally been looked at *through gun scopes* by hunters trying to figure out "*what I was* up in that tree?" and believe me, I was glad I had my orange on because without it, who knows what those morons would have done or what might have happened if they simply 'touched' their trigger. To find out exactly what a State requires in hunter orange, go to the internet and look up the requirements – remember, it is always better to be safe than to be sorry. Here are a couple sites to review:
*www.ncsl.org/programs/natres/orangehunt.htm*
*www.ihea.com/stateinfo/hunter-orange-req.php*

Ok, on to some detailed areas that are going to require camouflage as well. Your FEET! Camouflaged boots may seem like going a little overboard, but paying close attention to detail will result in more successful hunting. For the tree-stand hunter, your feet are sticking out there for the deer to see, first thing, and they provide nothing less than a solid blob for approaching game to visualize, and this, once again, is not a good idea. Even pant legs that ride up a hunter's legs and show the tops of his white tube socks can be enough to spook a trophy buck from coming any closer. Camouflage socks are

not going too far in my book if you want to
hunt for success.

Now, equipment: The hard surfaces of
hunting hardware, particularly traditional
blued steel (gun barrels) and finished
wood (gun stocks), typically have a sheen
to them that can actually "flash" reflected
sunlight and spook game. Would you turn
a flashlight on if a deer was approaching?
I didn't think so. Therefore, patterns are
also available in adhesive and slide-on
kits for concealing your weapon and other
hunting equipment while in the woods.

So, with all of that said, let me give you a
few short tips to set you on your way:

**Stay close to the cover you are trying
to blend into**. Don't "skyline" yourself
(show yourself as a silhouette against the
sky) on the tops of ridges and hills. The
best way to avoid this is to consciously
walk around in a way that keeps you
from being noticed against the plain sky.
Stay in the shadows; don't "spotlight"
yourself (making yourself look like you're
sitting under a stage light) by sitting out
in a sunny spot. Use every advantage
the habitat gives you to enhance your
camouflage effect and hide out in
shadows and other inconspicuous places.
Remember, you are in *their* living room

and they are going to notice what is out of place immediately.

**Keep your camouflage clothing clean** of all foreign odors. This is particularly important for hunters that hunt smell-sensitive game like the whitetail deer. Wash your clothing (and yourself) in no-scent soap products. No-scent or a neutral scent is best because this way you can add whatever cover, sex, or food scent product that is natural to a certain area and time of year to your garments to assist in attracting deer and covering up your own personal scent which is foreign to their 'home'.

PERSONAL STORY
*I had a friend who had asked me a few months prior to the hunting season if I would take him hunting with me. He didn't want to hunt himself, but he wanted to "hang out" with me and see how it was done. I agreed and told him that I would be by to pick him up at 4:00am sharp on the opening day of early bow season.*

*Upon pulling up to his house in my truck, I noticed that his bathroom light was on so I figured he was finishing up getting ready and he would be out shortly, so I just stayed in my truck and waited.*

*As it turned out, he took longer than I had anticipated and under the warmth of the truck's heater, I nodded off into a shallow sleep pattern only to be awakened by the slamming of my truck door and the pungent aroma of aftershave, deodorant and shampoo. He smelled like aisle 13 at the local Wal-Mart and I immediately bailed out of the truck rolling onto the ground as I landed. He looked at me and said, "What the heck are you doing?" As nicely as I could, I ordered him out of my truck and back into his house to take another shower with NO SOAPS OR DEODERANTS this time. I also told him to CHANGE CLOTHES, and told him he only had 5 minutes to do it all in. When he came back out, before I would even let him in my truck, I sprayed him down with a 'scent-blocker' and I mean I COATED HIM!! He thought I was nuts, but hey, this guy had never hunted in his life and he had no idea how important this was (my mistake for not discussing it with him prior to our hunt I guess – but I usually hunt alone so I never really had this problem).*

**Be alert for camouflage "washout".** Some camouflage fabrics eventually fade with both age and too many washes in the ol' washtub. A faded camouflage pattern loses both color and contrast and this undermines its ability to present the visual confusion necessary for effective camouflage cover. At some point you need to start over with new clothes for your camouflage to be at its peak performance.

**TIP:** *To delay fading as long as possible, wash your clothes turned inside out and in cold water - hang them outside to air dry.*

Good camouflage can allow you to get away with small, slow, and subtle movements, but take this advice: the best chance you have of going undetected is to always wait until the deer either looks away or its line of sight is obstructed somehow either by its passing by a tree or having its head down while it is eating. Then and only then should you make the necessary move to either stand, raise your weapon, or draw your bow. Believe me, no matter how good your camouflage is, you can defeat it by excessive movement while in sight of a deer. The result? As with most game animals, whether they are extremely color-sensitive (like turkeys) or nearly color-blind (like our deer), they can spot a flash of movement instantly, and when they do, they go somewhere else very quickly. Once this happens you will fully understand the concept of not moving while you are in the presence of deer.

## What Type Of Area Should I Hunt?

The best advice I can give to you when it comes to picking out your hunting area is to always keep in mind that deer are usually going to be where they eat. This means that **you should scout your area prior to the hunting season to see what pathways deer are taking to and from their feeding grounds and then plan your tree stand or ground blind location based on these travel patterns**. Also, during your scouting, remember to look for deer signs such as rubs, scrapes, droppings, etc. These will help confirm that deer are in the area and by the freshness of these signs, how often they are there. Study these signs often (we will cover 'deer signs' a bit later).

## How Do I Get Deer To Come To Me?

This is one of the most asked questions of new hunters so I am going to spend some time here discussing this - pay attention.

Unfortunately, unlike whistling for a trained dog to come to you, deer do not act in the same manner, but **you can plant some very enticing sounds and aromas into the air to lure them into your area**. This doesn't always work. They have to be the right smells and the right sounds at the right time to work.

**Scent Attractants** are used to attract deer into your area by tricking them into thinking that there are other deer where you are. One of the most prominent scent attractants used is the "Doe In Heat" scent that is used during the rutting stage. This scent is remarkably accurate to the same scent that a doe in estrous (in heat) will secrete while she is looking for a male deer (buck) to mate with. It is a pheromone that male deer can not pass up and if they get wind of it, they will surely head your way to find that doe that is calling to them to mate. It's instinctive.

**Deer Calls** are used to "talk" to the deer within range of hearing your call. Deer use a wide variety of vocalizations to communicate with each other under varying circumstances and studies have shown that there are up to 20 different types of sounds that a whitetail deer will make. However, there are only about 6 calls that you need to know as a hunter. Due to the fact that there are a number of different call-making devices on the market from hundreds of manufacturers, I am going to expose just a few of these to you and when to use them. It is always advisable to pick up a VHS or DVD on deer calling to watch and 'listen' closely on how to make the correct sound for the appropriate situation. Here are the 6 most frequently used calls that deer make:

* <u>Aggressive or Combative Call</u> – A low grunt sound that both the buck and the doe make year round. It is a close-contact call that is used to alert the other deer that they are too close and should back away. For this call, you should purchase what is commonly known as a "grunt tube".

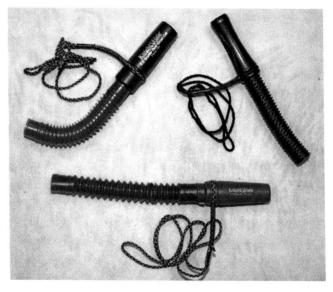

* <u>Tending Grunt Call</u> – This call is used by sexually excited males that are tending to their mates (does in heat). The buck will travel just behind the doe with his nose pretty much up her behind chasing and

licking her hind quarters until she finally decides to surrender to the dominant buck who wants to mate with her now. The sound is that of a pig who is rooting around in its pen foraging for food. You can recreate this sound with a "grunt tube" as well.

* <u>Alarm Snort Call</u> – This call is the one that most hunters are most familiar with because it is very loud and very alarming. It is when a deer is spooked and they blow a heavy amount of air through their nostrils with their mouth closed as they exit the area rapidly. It is usually used when they have either smelled or heard something 'out of the ordinary' in their living room but have not yet seen what it is, and as we know, they don't wait around to find out what it is either.

Usually 3-5 short 'blows' followed by some hoof pounding are what the hunter hears, and by this time he should know he is the reason the deer is alarmed. As a hunter this is very important to be able to recognize because it is a tell-tale sign that you have either chosen a poor stand location that can be detected easily, or that you are emitting an odor that the deer are onto. In either case, you want to be able to recognize this sound in the woods. If you hear it while hunting, you can pretty much count on your area being 'busted' or 'exposed' for the rest of that day. It may be time to pack it in or move.

* <u>Maternal Bleat</u> – The maternal bleat call is one that is used by fawns and young deer when they are trying to get the attention of their mother. It is a soft, high-pitched sound that is typically heard when a mother's offspring has been separated from her and they are calling out for help to locate her again. You might find an adult doe use this sound from time to time to alert tending bucks that they are ready to be mated with, but it is most commonly used by the yearlings in search of their mother. This sound can be recreated fairly easily, and for this, you can purchase either a hand-held bleat call that you blow into, or what I typically use is a 'bleat can' that you turn upside down and then back over again, thus emitting the bleat sound.

\* <u>Contact Call</u> – This is your most common call you will be using as it is the type of call which can be made year round but seems to be most effective in the early part of the season when bucks are still held up in their bachelor groups. It is basically a call (from a "grunt tube") that tells the bucks in the surrounding area, "Where are you? I'm over here – come here." It is very important to realize that you CAN overcall a deer. Don't get too aggressive with the grunt tube during this time. A few short blasts at a random spacing will tell the deer where you are, and whatever you do, if you see a buck headed in your direction, put the call down and stop calling - you have succeeded in bringing him in, now let him come in and look for 'you'. If you continue to call, he will pinpoint you and then focus on trying to 'wind you' (smell you) and you do NOT want him to do this because eventually he WILL and then he will be gone after he does. Call just enough to get him to come in, and then get ready to prepare to take the shot when he is within range.

\* <u>Snort-Wheeze Call</u> – If you are ever privileged enough to hear this sound in the woods it will be sure to send chills up your spine. I have only been fortunate enough to hear this sound on three occasions;

once while two bucks were actually fighting, and twice while a buck was warning another buck that he was about to mate and if he didn't leave the area at once, he was going to kick his butt right then and there! This happens usually right when a buck is playing a cat and mouse game with a doe he wants to breed and she has given in to his request.

It is caused when he rapidly exhales and inhales air simultaneously creating a sound that is so unique you will be sure to recognize it when you hear it. The only time I will ever recreate this sound in the woods is when I am in the middle of a heavy 'buck fight-simulation' where I am rattling horns together imitating two bucks locked up and having a shoving match. Then and *only* then will I even *consider* emitting some snort-wheeze calling into my rattling procedure, but not always.

\* <u>Rattling</u> – I know, I said there were only six, but I thought I had better touch on this type of calling since I mentioned it during the Snort-Wheeze section.

Contrary to what many hunters think, I believe that antler rattling will work anywhere you can find whitetail deer. After all, they are somewhat like us in nature and if someone is trying to horn in on our girl, aren't we going to be willing to fight them for her? Absolutely. So, with that in mind, let's discuss antler rattling.

Antler rattling has been around for hundreds of years when Indians used to smack dried-out sticks together to get deer to present themselves within range for a shot. What antler rattling consists of is taking two sheds (one side of a  deer's rack found in the woods), or prefabricated sheds (like these purchased from a hunting supply store), or nowadays, a 'rattling bag' (see next page) and making it sound like two mature bucks are locking horns and trying to push and shove the other one to the ground.

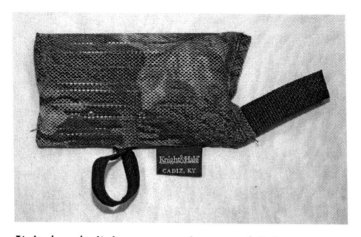

It is loud; it is aggressive; and it is effective during the rutting period. It occurs in the wild when one deer that is usually not the alpha buck in his area decides he wants to challenge the alpha buck to a 'dual' for "control rights". This is when heads collide and the effect can be quite a site if you are fortunate enough to ever see it. It is a fight that either ends up with one of the bucks running off in fear, or in death as the dominant buck shoves his opponent to the ground and gores him to death with his own rack. It is nothing short of a brutal fist-fight you might witness somewhere when two grown men are fighting without abandon for the hand of a young woman. It is ugly, and it is seemingly uncalled for, and although it doesn't happen often, when it does, it is a matter of respect, dignity, and power – just like it is for humans most of the time.

**TIP:** *Another call I often use during early bow season is a 'turkey call'. This allows me to fool 'listening deer' into thinking I am nothing more than an innocent turkey scratching around in the leaves for food, when in reality, I am a hunter walking to my deer stand. How you ask? Walk a little – scratch around – give a few clucks, and then move on a little further and repeat.*

## Should I Worry About Being Detected?

There's not a whole lot more I can say here. **We have talked about how important it is not to be detected by smell; sight; and sound while in the woods.** If you take heed to all of these warnings and study various methods on how to avoid being detected in these areas, you will undoubtedly blend into your surroundings and thus increase your chances of sighting more deer during your hunting excursion without being detected.

## How Do I Know When I Am Ready?

There is only one way to know if you are ready to hunt whitetail deer. **You and only you will know if you are accurate with your weapon of choice (you can never practice too much); legal by obtaining all of the proper licenses (and other requirements to meet regulatory standards for your area);**

**and have done your homework to know basically what you are doing (before, during, and after the hunt).**

If you are uncomfortable in any of these areas, then you are not ready to begin hunting as all of these factors must be in place in order for you to succeed in the woods when it really counts. I hear way too many times of hunters who never see any deer; or hunters who miss their intended target; or hunters who don't know what they are going to do with the deer after they have killed it. BE PREPARED before you set out to kill something. You owe it to yourself, but more importantly, you owe it to the deer and the sport of ethical deer hunting.

# Chapter Three

# DURING THE HUNT

**FAST FACT**
**I want to stress that it is very important to be totally 'in-tune' with all of your surroundings during the hunt. You can never be over-prepared.**

Be sure you are watching intently; listening to every sound you hear; analyzing wind direction and speed; searching for any little movement that might catch the corner of your eye; etc. Talk to any deer hunter and they will tell you – when you let down your guard is when the deer will suddenly appear right before your eyes out of nowhere. Chances are, when this happens, you won't be ready to take the shot and they won't stick around and wait for you to get ready.

## What Time Should I Plan To Hunt?

As we have previously discussed, deer typically travel to their feeding areas from their bedding areas in the *last* few minutes of daylight. On the return trip they travel from their feeding areas to their bedding areas in the *first* few minutes of daylight. **In most States you are allowed to hunt during a time period that ranges**

**from 30 minutes before sunrise until 30 minutes after sunset. This one hour time period is one of the most productive time of the day to hunt whitetail deer**. Many hunters seem to avoid this hour of daylight by wanting 'light' in order to travel to their stand or back to their vehicle in, so they can see. Wah! I guess it's just not *convenient* for them. Well, I'm here to tell you, if you want convenience, then take up a video game because there is nothing convenient about deer hunting. But, if a hunter is going to waste an hour of their hunting day for convenience sake, then I'm all for it because they are going to miss out on the best time to hunt and that just leaves them for me. Seriously though, this is NOT the hour you want to choose to be traveling around – this is the hour you should already be set up and hunting.

PERSONAL STORY
*A friend of mine was over at my studio one day and he was looking at all of the game I had in my game room that I had taken myself. Totally overwhelmed, he asked me, "How in the world do you get all of these things?" I simply answered him with the facts of a hunter's life, stating all of the preparatory work I do during the preseason; all of the time I spend in the*

*woods during the rain, and the snow, and the bitter cold; the patience I display when it comes to the end of a day and having not seen any game or not gotten off a shot; etc. Do you know what he said to me after that? He said, "I would love to have a room like this but there is no way I could sit in the woods that long in poor weather conditions, it just wouldn't be worth it to me."*

He was exactly right! It is all a matter of what is most important to you. You either have it, or you don't. What I am talking about is the desire to hunt or not. It's not a video game that you can turn on and off anytime you want while in the comfort of your easy chair. It is a commitment of the mind, the body, and most of all, the heart. It's not easy, no one said it was. But it is a requirement if you want continued success.

Even if you have the biggest heart for hunting in the entire woods, a deer's behavior is not preset for your desires. They have a mind of their own and it is only your own determination and commitment that will grant you eventual success. And I DID say, "eventual". Heck, I never even SAW a deer for the first 2 years I hunted and never got a shot off on one (which I missed by the way) for the first 7 years I hunted. That in itself was enough to make most quit long before I finally even got to take a stupid shot! But I was different – I wanted it bad. It literally sickens me to hear of someone who has done nothing to prepare for a hunt other than purchase a hunting license, deer tag, and borrowed someone's shotgun, to have gone out and killed a buck their first time out, and then brag about how easy it is. Ask this same person five years afterwards if they did that every year – the answer will most-likely be "no" unless they are hunting within some fenced-in preserve somewhere and then *that* isn't hunting.

Yes, deer are creatures of habit, but at the same time their behavior can easily be altered by several factors. The most common of these are typically precipitation, wind, hunting pressure, and the rut. Deer will usually stay in their bedding areas during times of heavy rain or snow but when the storm stops they will start moving around for a couple of reasons:

- The trees and brush are usually dripping with wetness and this noise will make the deer nervous because they can't hear any danger that may be approaching, so they will move about and go to 'visual surveillance'.

- They will also start moving if the storm lasted through their feeding period. This is when their travel patterns are going to be used from their bedding areas to their feeding areas at an unpredictable time, so be awake. Know these and hunt these hard after a long storm.

Keep in mind that although windy days in the woods can be very dangerous for deer, they can also be very dangerous for hunters as well. The wind can cause tree limbs to fall and even weak trees to topple over. If you choose to hunt on windy days, please be sure to use extra caution. I have been hit by limbs in the past and was even in a tree one time when it decided to uproot and start over – luckily it caught on an adjacent tree and stopped just after it got started, but I was definitely looking for a soft landing area to bail to if it came to that point (totally forgetting that I was strapped to the tree itself with my safety harness). Not a very pleasant feeling knowing you are going down and there is nothing you can do about it. God was with me that day and I am grateful for His intervention. God is good – ALL the time!

Also, deer hunters roaming through the woods will cause deer to move from their bedding areas so keep a keen eye on the woods or your hunting area during 'lunch time'. For the life of me, I will never understand why so-called hunters feel it is necessary to leave their stands to go to their vehicles to eat their lunches. I personally will not come down out of my stand until about an hour after sunset. Once I'm up there, I STAY up there! Hunters traveling back and forth to their vehicles during the lunch hours have pushed some pretty nice deer into my sights over the years and I would like to take this opportunity to personally thank them for their need to eat in their vehicle.

**The rut is the period of time when bucks mate with does**. The overall rut period usually lasts about 4-6 weeks and in most parts of the country occurs in November - although this does vary depending on geographic location. During the rut all deer are more active, especially the bucks. It is not unusual to see a buck chasing a doe during the middle of the day when they are normally resting. It can be easily said that the rut clouds a buck's judgment as they are often seen doing things they wouldn't normally do. I have heard stories of similar behavior occurring at local 'pick up spots' and the simple fact is: male animals are male animals - regardless of how many legs they walk on or what they look like.

One last factor that many hunters rely on when hunting, is the position of the moon. Most of you have probably heard that the position of the moon plays a big part in the activity of fish. Well, the moon also seems to have a direct effect on deer movement. I believe that the amount of "light" that the moon projects is what actually triggers the rutting period, and like we just said, with the rut comes deer movement. So watch the moon as well.

## **Stand Hunting Or Ground Hunting?**

WOW! This is SO varied that it is going to be very tough to help you here. There are many arguments for both sides of this discussion, but since I am the one writing this book, I will give you MY view on this topic. **STAND HUNT any time you can!** Why? Because the higher you are in a tree, the less likely a deer is going to locate you. How many times have you seen a calm deer walking through the woods looking 'up'? Never, right? However, if you are on the ground, you are now eye-level with the deer and everything about you is eye-level; and nose-level; and ear-level. I tend to hunt either 20'-0 high in a ladder stand that has been out all year (so the deer get used to it being there) or my favorite is my backpack climbing tree stand (that my beautiful wife purchased for me a few years ago) and I can put anywhere I want anytime I go out. With this stand, I usually climb anywhere from 20'-0 to 30'-0 high depending on what the wind is doing that day. And I don't come down until I'm DONE! You need to stay up there all day so get a stand that is comfortable. It's worth it.

**TIP**: *The best place for stand placement is anywhere there is an updraft in the woods near a travel route. Look for those little 'tornadoes' while you are out scouting in the off-season. Placing a stand in this area will draw your scent upward rather than blow it out and downward for the deer to smell. Works for me – and if it works for me, I'm not going to change a thing.*

# BASIC TREE STAND TYPES

**typical "Lock-On" Tree Stand**

**typical "Ladder" Tree Stand**

**author's "Climber" Tree Stand**

As I have stated before, I prefer a climber because you can take it anywhere and use it anywhere you can find a straight tree. Even if you don't find a straight tree, you can always climb the tree and mount it wherever you want regardless of how you get up there just as you would a lock-on stand, and climbers are more comfortable.

But if you *do* find a tree to climb, here is how you use your climber stand to reach your desired height. It is very simple and requires little effort and strength.

# HOW TO USE A CLIMBER STAND

First you sit down and face the tree, locking your feet in the straps.

Then you stand up and pull the seat portion up with you as you stand.

Next you sit down again and pull your feet up to your stomach raising the lower platform. Then you stand back up and repeat the entire process as you go up the tree. It's very easy and you use very little muscle. It is nothing more than standing up and sitting down time and time again, and you can climb as high as you want (or need to) with very little effort. This helps keep your 'sweat scent' to a minimal level which is very important when it comes to deer hunting, remember?

It is always wise to purchase a stand that you will be comfortable in ALL DAY LONG – like this one. This is my own personal climber stand and you can see just how comfortable it really is. I can easily stay in it all day long. Important - remember?

As you can also tell from this photo, it is very versatile and safe, as well as quiet. I can move around in my stand without making a noise which of course is *very* important also - remember?

## <u>When Do I Take The Shot?</u>
### *TO SHOOT or NOT TO SHOOT?*

*That* seems to be the million dollar question that every hunter asks, so listen closely. When you are contemplating on whether to shoot or not, **the first thing you must consider is whether or not your shot can hit the vital area (kill zone) of the deer without any interference.** If not, then you should not take the shot. Even if you think you 'might' hit the vital area, it is not worth the work that is going to be required of you in tracking a wounded deer that can literally travel *miles* when injured. Be sure your shot placement is accurate and precise – you'll thank yourself later.

As you can see in the above picture, the circled area is the prime kill area called the 'vital zone' and this is where your shot should ALWAYS be placed. NOTE: If the front leg of the deer is 'back', then the shoulder may be protecting the vital area just a bit, so if you can, always wait until the front leg takes a step 'forward' to open up the vital area for a clean hit with good penetration through the vitals. (note where the vital organs are)

**NO SHOT –** This deer is alert and looking straight at you – don't even try it – it is a low-percentage shot and your chance of killing the deer is slim.

**YES, SHOOT –** This is the ideal position to take a shot on a deer – relaxed, looking away, vital area pretty clear of any obstruction, and ready for the taking! Take your time and squeeze gently on the trigger.

**NO SHOT –** Deer is behind brush and if you take this shot you are probably going to miss the vitals altogether and only succeed at killing a tree or a bush instead. No meat in trees dude, so relax and let him walk out first.

**NO SHOT –** Way too much meat and bone to go through to get to the vital area so don't even waste your ammo. You'll be tracking this deer for miles if you do shoot and probably will never recover it anyway. It will be meat for the coyotes.

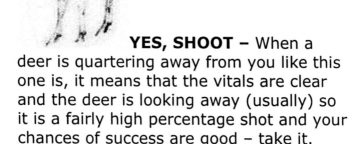

**YES, SHOOT –** When a deer is quartering away from you like this one is, it means that the vitals are clear and the deer is looking away (usually) so it is a fairly high percentage shot and your chances of success are good – take it.

**NO SHOT –** Are you kidding me? If you can hit the vital area while it is moving at 40mph you need to be on the Olympic skeet shooting team in lieu of deer hunting. Don't take a chance on just injuring the deer – always make a good decision to take a clean and ethical shot only. It's the right choice.

**YES, SHOOT –** This is a great angle for a shot – another quartering away shot, but you will need to aim a little behind the vital area to be sure that the line of travel of the ammunition you are using hits him in the vital area as it passes through. A bit trickier but you can do it if you have been 'practicing' as instructed.

**NO SHOT –** Why? Because again, we find brush in the way. If the brush is small, you 'might' succeed, but why take the chance? Let him walk out of the brush and *then* take him down.

**SHOT? MAYBE –** This is a walking shot that only the experienced and most confident of hunters should take as it is attempting to hit a moving target. It is always a shot that would be in question, especially if you aren't confident in your shooting abilities yet. Be sure first.

**NO SHOT –** Man-oh-man have I ever seen this enough times in my days. He is looking right at you – remember, he can't focus on you but if you move, he is gone. Be smart - stand still, wait for him to turn, and *then* shoot.

**YES, SHOOT –** If you have ever been up in a tree stand and had one walk under you, then you know this angle. Place your shot a little behind and a little high (toward spine) to inflict a fatal shot.

**NO SHOT –** Unless you are using armor-piercing ammo, there is no vital area exposed. NEVER take a neck or head shot – the percentage of success is way too low to take a chance, and once again, you will only wound the animal and probably never recover it.

Some of the best advice I received from an old hunting buddy was this: "If you *think* that you can hit the vital area based on your ability and the deer's location, then you probably should NOT shoot." Why? Because if you only THINK that you can hit it means that you are not SURE you can hit it, and therefore it is not a high percentage shot and should be passed on. I always try and make sure that when I am setting up my stand that I clear out any debris that might be in the way of a clear shot when the time comes. *Be careful here though, you don't want to clear out too much or you will blow your cover.* A little goes a long way for clearing a shooting lane right where you need it. After all, you are going to be poised in that spot as the deer is approaching anyway.

**TIP**: *If a deer is walking and you need it to stop in a certain spot to take a shot, you can either whistle or just say, "Hey" and the deer's own curiosity will more than likely stop it dead in its tracks long enough for you to get the shot off. I personally do a low grunt with my 'mouth' (not a call) and this seems to work fine most of the time.*

# Chapter Four

## AFTER THE SHOT

**FAST FACT**
**Inevitably, the biggest mistake that hunters make after taking the shot is not watching which direction the deer heads into the woods after being shot. The second biggest mistake is chasing after it too soon. Be patient and wait.**

**After I Shoot What Do I Do?**
**After you have *made* the shot on the deer, it is important to watch the path that the deer takes if it runs off.** Make a mental note of the last place you see the deer so you can go to that spot and mark it once you are down out of your tree stand or up out of your ground blind.

If you missed, then just sit tight. Watch the deer's posture, and maybe give a few short 'contact grunts' to see if he will circle back out of curiosity as to what just happened. Deer 'want' to know where their danger is at all times and many times they will circle back around in an attempt to locate it before relaxing for the day.

But for purposes here, we are going to assume that you have 'practiced' enough (notice how that word keeps popping up?) and your shot was on the money.

First, be sure your Hunter Orange is visible. You don't want to be shot at while walking around looking for your deer by some idiot in the woods that can't tell the difference in man and deer (it happens).

Now, go directly to the spot you last saw the deer and <u>mark this spot</u> with some surveyor's flagging tape. After you have done so, go ahead and pack up your gear. I usually take mine back to my vehicle and give the wounded deer plenty of time to relax and lie down. Following it too soon would only push it further into the woods and if you have ever had to drag a deer out of the woods by yourself, the closer it is to your vehicle the better off you will be for sure. If the deer is already down within sight of where you shot it, skip the next step and go to 'Once I Find The Deer What Do I Do?' and follow the instructions there.

## If The Deer Runs Off What Do I Do?
Ok, this is where patience and preparation will persevere. If you have prepared for a successful recovery by packing along a watch, notepad, pencil, compass, surveyor tape and high-beam spotlight, then your chances of recovering your deer are much greater. The first four items are required

to document what happens immediately after you shoot and the rest for actually tracking the deer through the woods.

*During* the shot, try and 'see' where your shot enters the deer at. If you have done your homework and practiced diligently (there's that word again), you should have a pretty good idea as it will be close to where you aimed. This is why practice is so important before the hunt itself – it saves you much time during the recovery period of your downed deer because you already have a pretty good idea of what area you hit on the deer and how bad it is hurt. Also, <u>right after the shot</u>, try and 'listen' to the sound your arrow or your slug makes as it hits the deer. See if you can hear the broadhead of the arrow pass through cleanly or hit bone. It is understandably more difficult to hear the slug because your ears are still ringing from the shot blast. This is why it is important to attempt to 'see' the hit.

**When a deer flees, listen to the noises that it makes as it runs through the woods.** Make note of what you hear, as well as what direction the deer ran listening closely to see if it staggered and fell, or kept running. The longer you can hear the animal in the woods, the farther it is probably traveling and the longer it will take to locate. Write all that you can hear down – it will help you later.

Now, immediately after the shot, catch your breath and record the time of the shot and the direction the deer fled. Check your compass and mark it down as direction could play an important role later if you get turned around in the woods. Sit tight and keep your composure. I know you will want to jump down and chase after the deer, but inexperienced hunters mistakenly climb down too quickly to recover their game and thus push the wounded animal further into the woods making it more difficult to track.

Unfortunately, all shots are not clean kills. When liver or gut-shots occur, pushing the animal can be disastrous. Jumped too quickly after they have laid down to die, a deer will often get a "second breath" and can sometimes cover over a mile before stopping again. This is why it is so important to let the animal lay down without fear of someone chasing it. Eventually, it will not be able to get back to its feet and thus bleed out and expire.

So, while you are patiently waiting, try and recall how the animal reacted to the shot. Missed deer usually run away, but so do those that have been shot through the heart and/or the lungs. One that prances off could mean a miss. Deer kicking high like a bucking horse usually indicates a vital area hit (good shot), while those that run off with arched backs or with their tail tucked in are often gut-shot (bad shot).

Wait 30 to 45 minutes before leaving your tree stand. This is a good time to pack up your gear and get it ready to transport. After all, you are leaving so there is no need not making use of this time wisely.

Once on the ground it is time to begin the tracking process. Gather all the evidence you can by logging it onto your notepad. Go to where the animal was shot. Are there blood spots or splatters? Is it a lot or a little? Is fluid other than blood present? If bow hunting, recovering the arrow is key. Fluids or substances other than blood on an arrow shaft can reveal if the animal was gut shot or liver shot. If this is the case, you will need to wait longer; it may take 4 to 6 hours for the deer to perish, so wait 3 to 4 hours before you begin tracking the blood trail any further. If it is late in the evening, it may be best to come back early in the morning with some friends, but if you have the time to spare before dark, then take the time to haul all of your gear back to your vehicle and grab a bite to eat to help pass the time.

Ok, time has passed, now it's time to continue. Keep in mind that following a blood trail can be very tricky. First, mark the initial blood spot with a long strip of bright-orange surveyor's tape tied well above the ground for visibility from long distances. I usually grab a young sapling and bend it over and tie it to the top, then once I release it, it is high above where I can see it (and please don't try and climb a small sapling to do this, it will be very embarrassing for you even if no one is looking). Now, in your notepad, record the compass direction. As you travel along following the drops of blood you find, every 40-50 yards tie surveyor's tape above these drops so you will be able to 'look back' and make a determination as to the deer's travel path. <u>Do not walk on the blood trail</u>. If you need to start over later, a walked-upon blood trail can be useless and make it even more difficult to track when there is less light to depend on.

Accurately reading a blood trail requires time spent tracking. Each tracking chore is unique. Easy-to-follow 'heavy' blood trails occur when primary blood vessels are severed. These are in the carotid artery of the neck; the pyloric artery behind the stomach paunch; the aortic artery under the spine; or the hindquarter's femoral artery. All of these can be gushers.

## PERSONAL STORY

*I was hunting over the edge of a field at a good friend of mine's farm and I was up in my stand about 25 feet in the air. I was hunting for meat and had lured a large doe to my area. As I watched her come closer, she eventually walked directly under my stand. As I drew my bow, I had to be careful not to shoot my own foot because she was that far directly under me. When I released the arrow, I heard a big "whoosh" and at the same time felt like someone had just sprayed me lightly with a water hose. The doe bolted and as she ran I could see her shooting blood a long distance into the air so I knew I had hit the aortic artery just under her spine. After she was out of sight, I went back to the sound I heard when I shot to help in my tracking needs, and suddenly noticed I was covered in blood. I had hit the artery so clean that it immediately erupted straight up the arrow shaft and hit ME - 25 feet up in the air! There was blood dripping from the leaves; from my stand; even from the bill of my cap. I had never seen anything like this before but soon came to realize that a deer can still run a long way even with this amount of severe blood loss and trauma. I eventually found her near a creek bed (many deer will head toward water when gut-shot also) about 150 yards from the point of contact.*

A point to remember is that not all mortally-wounded deer immediately spill blood; however, a hard-hit deer typically leaves blood no farther than 15 to 25 yards from where they were initially shot. This is why I stress that you should watch which direction the deer runs off to after the shot so you can get a good idea of which direction you will be heading.

The color and condition of the blood is also important and sometimes reveals the type of hit that was inflicted upon the deer. Bright-red is a great sign, usually indicating an oxygen-rich artery has been clipped. Pinkish, frothy (bubbly) blood usually indicates a good lung hit. Easy-to-follow dark-red droplets that disappear after a couple hundred yards often indicate a muscle shot. Chances of recovering a deer that has been muscle-shot are low, but not impossible so don't give up – keep looking. You may find more signs of the deer bleeding out later.

Be alert for blood where you don't expect it, and take your time - be observant. Understand that wounds do not always bleed externally and that blood trails often disappear. Many times your tracking efforts will move from following a blood trail to following nothing. This is a critical point in the tracking process. Remember when I said that you will be tying off surveyor's tape for a reason? Well, now is the time to look back at your tape trail and slowly move in the charted direction. Be alert for sign other than blood. Overturned leaves, hoof prints, trampled grass, and leaves pressed flat when a deer lies down. All of these should be searched for.

I usually recommend a "circle search" when a blood trail is exhausted. It is actually more of a 'spiral search' but that is just me being anal. Either way, such a search starts where the last sign was marked, expanding from the center with each circle. This works best with a two to three man effort but can also work with just you. I have found many deer after losing a blood trail by using the circle method.

Here is how it works: think of a coil on an electric range top – you are in the middle and now you are going to start circling outward.

Do this until you are about 75-100 yards from your starting point. If you don't find anything now, start it again – I'm sure you have missed or just plain overlooked something that was there. After all, a deer doesn't 'fly' so it had to leave some sign somewhere. If you still can't find any, it's probably safe to say that making a living as a Game Tracker or CSI Agent probably aren't in your career future – HA! Go get some help – someone will find something!

It is tough to find a buck during daylight when there's very little blood, and night recovery is far more difficult, but it can be done if you are persistent and thorough. Large flashlights, such as the hand-held beacon-type spotlight I use, project a bright beam and are a *must* to carry. My friend Mark, who wrote the 'Foreword' section of this book, likes to use a Coleman lantern, but I have always been afraid of setting the woods on fire so I don't go that route (ha!). A bright, blinding light is great for illuminating wide areas of ground, and will actually make blood drops appear to glow or shine out.

Make sure you know the local hunting laws when trailing deer at night. Some States prohibit carrying a firearm or bow in the woods along with a light after legal shooting hours, but to be perfectly honest with you, after being pinned down by coyotes on two separate occasions (one even as I tried to recover my *own* deer), you will rarely find me without 'something' in my boot or back pocket for my own personal protection. My life is worth a fine if it comes down to that – but you didn't hear that from me, ok? (sssshhhhhh).

Once you have come to the end of the blood trail and you have yet to locate your downed game, there is only one other method that might work, but, it will take 8-10 more people to even have a chance. It is called a "grid search."

Using a compass, line people in a row, arm-length apart, to go in one direction. The searchers must be close enough to one another to be able to clearly see the feet of the person on either side. The line of people then moves slowly through the woods searching for the deer. After going 50 to 100 yards, or reaching a barrier such as a fence or a road, the line "flip-flops", then moves across the same tract again. If the deer is not in this vicinity, then you head in another direction based on the compass. This is repeated back and forth through the woods until a grid has been thoroughly searched. And don't count out areas across the road or creek either – a deer is hurt and scared – it will cross ANYTHING to get away. After listening to hunters who have used the grid system for recovery everywhere from New York to Colorado, I have yet to hear of it fail to turn up a lost deer - eventually. It just takes more manpower and more time to do it this way.

Unfortunately, sooner or later most hunters face the frustration of losing a trail or having it dry up or get washed out because of rain or other factors, and although we hate to admit failure, we have to be sensible enough to know when it is time to give up the search. My rule of thumb is this: If you don't find your game within 48 hours from the time of the shot, chances are you won't, and by this time other predators have already received your game for themselves, graciously I might add, so even if you do find it, there won't be much left to take home anyway.

IF YOU HAVE SHOT A MONSTER BUCK AND LOST HIM – you can still probably recover the rack within a few days. Just go back out and watch for buzzards. They will help you locate what is left of your deer. But if you wait too long, the squirrels and other small game will feed off of the rack for calcium and it will be long gone also.

So, with all of that said, let's do everything we can to recover the animals that we shoot. We owe it to them; we owe it to each other; and we owe it to the Gaming administration; ethical hunting FIRST!

## **Once I Find The Deer What Do I Do?**

After you see your animal lying on the ground you need to **make sure it is dead**. Approach the animal from *behind* with your gun or bow aimed at the animal just in case it starts to get up. There is nothing more dangerous than a wounded and scared animal – especially if it has horns. Make sure the animal is completely expired before you get any closer to it. One way to make sure that your deer is in fact deceased is to take a stick and touch the deer's eye with it. Now don't go and poke it out dufus – that would just be sick – just lightly touch it. If the deer has any life left in it at all, it will not be able to tolerate this sensation and will blink or flinch. If this happens and the deer is NOT dead, it is highly recommended that you make another shot into the vital area of the deer's chest. DO NOT attempt to slice open the deer's throat with a knife just to save a bullet or arrow – this will get you laid up in a hospital faster than you can scream because a deer's hooves are extremely swift and extremely deadly. If it is a buck, and it can get up at all, its antlers will lay you wide open. So be the smart hunter and just shoot the deer again. It's okay. They make more ammo.

Now, if your deer is dead and you have confirmed this by using the method as described above, then it is time to take care of paperwork. Yes, you heard me right – just like at the office – there is paperwork to do so read this carefully!

Most States require that you carry a special license specifically designed for this time of the hunt. This special license is called a 'tag' and it is used to identify a variety of data that is very useful in the field of Wildlife Conservation.

### The Tag Identifies The Following:
1)   You - the hunter who killed the deer
2)   What type of deer you killed
3)   What weapon you used
4)   What the kill date was

In some States you are required to note this information on a 'Temporary Transportation Tag' and then affix the tag to a part of the deer before moving it. Be sure to consult your local laws and regulations for proper tagging procedures of harvested game as they vary from State-to-State.

Ok, now that you understand what a tag is and what it is used for, let's look at one. On the next page is a sample tag for you to review. These tags, once again, vary from State-to-State so be careful to read it thoroughly before filling it out.

## Deer Temporary Transportation Tag (Sample)

**Online license temporary tag instructions**

▪ This sample tag, or a piece of paper including your name, address and date the deer was taken, must be attached to the leg of the deer immediately after taking the deer.

▪ Write your deer hunting license number on the tag.

▪ Upon killing a deer, immediately mark the tag with the month and the date of the kill, and the sex of the deer.

▪ You are not required to have the tag attached to the deer while dragging it from the field, but you must tag it before you load it in a vehicle or leave it unattended.

▪ Deer must be checked at a deer check-in station within 48 hours of taking.

---------------------- Cut Along Dotted Line ----------------------

*DNR Online License (Complete before hunting)*

**Indicate License Type**

? Regular deer license

? Bonus antlerless license

? Military or refuge license

**Online License Number** _____

**Indicate License Season**

? Archery

? Extra Archery

? Firearm

? Muzzleloader

***Mark sex and date of kill (Complete after the kill)***

? Resident ? Non-resident

? Male ? Female

? Oct ? Nov ? Dec ? Jan

*(Circle the date of the kill)*

1 2 3 4 5 6 7 8 9 10 11 12 13 14 15 16 17 18 19 20 21 22 23 24 25 26 27 28 29 30 31

So, let's assume that you have made the necessary notations and already 'tagged' the deer. Now you are ready to start the cleaning process. This is one step that I personally could easily pass on if I had a guide that would do it for me, but since most hunters are like me and they are their own guide, this dreaded task is always left up to the individual hunter to perform. Remember, your kill - your job.

## **Do I Have To Clean The Deer?**
**Yes! We call this process "field dressing" or by its more common name, "gutting" the deer.** It is not the most pleasant task but it has to be done in order to preserve the meat and to be able to haul the deer to your vehicle. Remember, deer weigh as much if not more than a human so the relativity of resistance is on the deer's side to begin with so don't complain, it will help you.

Field dressing takes some effort so your heavy hunting clothes should be removed so they won't be soiled with your own sweat and the deer's bodily fluids during the process. You do not want deer blood on your hunting clothes (due to the sensitive nature of the deer's sense of smell which they *will* pick up on during your next hunt). Many hunters go to their truck to change before dressing out their deer. I actually have a "Field Dress Kit" in a tackle box that I carry in my truck when I hunt for this very purpose. To better help you prepare, here is what I have in my own personal kit – you might want to write these down:

- A sharp hunting knife (for cutting anything other than what you will be cutting during the skinning process)

- A sharp skinning knife (mine is known as a 'Wyoming' knife)

- A small hatchet (for breaking the pelvic bone later, if needed)

- Rope (for tying the legs open so you can work on the deer)

- 4ea Tent Stakes (for help in tying the legs open)

- 2 pr of shoulder-length latex gloves (for protection during the process and yes, you WILL want them)

- Lightweight coveralls (for covering myself during the process)

- Surgical Booties (for covering my boots so I don't have to change)

- Flare (I carry a flare because once I was 'pinned down' by 3 coyotes while I was field dressing *my* deer – the flare is now used for scaring them off if I should be caught in that unfortunate position again)

- Small first-aid kit (you *will* cut yourself if you are not careful)

- Cell Phone (I know of a hunter who severed his own artery during this process when his knife slipped and stabbed his leg – his cell phone actually saved his life!) My cell phone even has a GPS locator system on it should I become unconscious and can't dial, I can still be found. I have it on there for this reason and this reason only.

There are many other things you can add to your field dressing kit, but this is most of what I have in mine. Once you do this a few times you may want to swap out things that work best for you. Again, this is what works for me so this is what I use.

## FIELD DRESSING YOUR DEER

Ok, now that we are all 'covered up' and ready to begin, let's get the deer in the proper position for the field dressing task.

**1)**    Roll the deer over on its back with the butt end of the deer lower than the head (it helps to find a slight incline to do this on) and spread the back legs. Take the rope and tie all four legs to surrounding trees or shrubs, and if you haven't any to tie to, use the hatchet and tent stakes in your field dressing kit now.

# STOP RIGHT HERE

***Before going any further -*** *you need to decide on whether or not you plan on having your deer head mounted for hanging on your wall. <u>If you are going to,</u> then you need to be sure to follow this next step before proceeding:*

## <u>Alternate Step Required If Mounting</u>

In order for the taxidermist to have enough hide in the chest area to produce a professional-looking mount, you will need to stop your cut up the belly to the chest area at the base of the ribcage! This will make cleaning out the entrails a little more difficult but it needs to be done in order to produce a nice shoulder mount.

With this noted, please continue on with step #2 of the field dressing process.

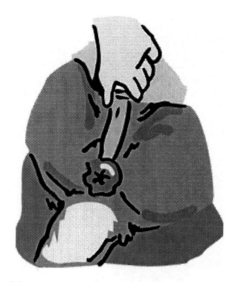

**2)**    I like to remove the deer's penis (if applicable) and anal opening first before going any further. I usually use a separate knife for this step in case I get some 'unwanted fluids' on it so as not to spoil the meat as I continue the field dressing task. Be careful NOT to cut through these organs – you want to cut 'around' them and then remove them. The mess you will avoid is well worth the extra effort to be very careful at this time.

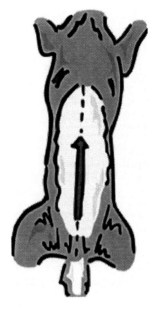

**3)** Once these are removed, working from the anus forward, begin cutting through the deer's hide and skin but <u>NOT ANY DEEPER</u>. You do not want to cut too deep and puncture the stomach area.

A way to avoid doing this by mistake is to make all of your cuts in an upward motion as if you were cutting the string on a package. Stabbing into the carcass is not a good idea because you will puncture things you don't want to puncture and the stench will literally knock you right off of your feet. Besides, you will have a mess that will not help this task in the least.

**4)**    Use your free hand to hold the stomach area down as you cut, and be extremely careful not to cut your fingers or your face! You can also hold open the cavity as you cut around the vital organs inside, but this will expose things that smell so try not to lean over the opening right off the bat – you will want to acclimate your senses to this first.

**5)** Now untie the deer and roll the animal onto its side and reach into the open cavity area (with your shoulder-length gloves on) and begin pulling the intestines and organs out of the cavity.

Go ahead and let them hit the ground – they won't be there in the morning...the coyotes, opossums, and other animals will feed on them throughout the night. (sick, I know, but hey, look at it as you're providing nourishment for other wildlife).

**6)** After you have pulled the majority of the entrails out of the deer, you will need to cut the tissue that holds the organs and intestines in place. Just pull them toward you and cut whatever is holding them in the carcass. <u>Be careful not to cut the entrails</u> as these will release fluids that will taint the meat as well as, once again, make your task very messy.

**7)**    Next, roll the animal onto the opposite side and repeat step 5 to ensure all of the membrane tissue has been removed from inside the carcass.

**8)**    Now you must straddle the deer and reach up into the throat of the deer and cut the deer's windpipe. It looks/feels like a vacuum cleaner hose and is the last thing holding the entrails in place. Reach as far up into the throat as you can and cut the windpipe. You can't see what you are doing so you have to feel your way around – be careful not to cut yourself here. Once you have made this cut, remove the remainder of the vital organs such as the lungs, the heart, and the liver.

**9)** Look over the deer and make sure you have cleaned out the cavity thoroughly. If you have done your job well, you will have much less of a mess once back at the house.

**10)** It's ok to take a breather for 5, 10, even 20 minutes once you have finished these steps. You will be tired and you will need to regain your strength for the next step that follows. Use this time to clean up your tools and other field dressing paraphernalia that you have used because you don't want to leave it in the woods!

## How Do I Get The Deer To My Vehicle?
Ok, the deer has been field dressed and your area is cleaned up of your gear and it is time to get the deer back to your vehicle. **There are items that can be purchased to assist in this laborious task, but most hunters choose just to drag the deer out**. If it is a buck the

task is a bit easier because you can use the antlers as a 'handle' to drag him by. If it is a doe, you will soon find out just how many times a deer can 'roll over' during the dragging process. Be sure that you are in good shape or get some help because this takes a toll on the ol' ticker. You could be susceptible to a heart attack if you're not careful. Take your time, work in short spurts, and don't overdue it - eventually you will reach your destiny. It's not a race and you shouldn't treat it as one.

Now, get your bearings straight on which way to your vehicle. There is nothing worse than dragging a 150-200 pound deer up and down hills and hollers and over fallen trees just to realize that you have been heading in the wrong direction.

**JOKE**: *Two hunters were dragging a deer through the woods when they noticed that limbs and brush and other debris kept getting lodged in the deer's antlers. Frustrated with the extra lag, one stated, "Hey, why don't we drag the deer from the other end so that stuff doesn't get caught in the antlers as we're draggin' him?" "Good idea" the other hunter said, and they started dragging the deer by the other end. "Man, this was a great idea – nothing is getting caught in the antlers*

*and it is so much easier to drag." "Yup"
answered the other hunter, "but the truck
keeps getting farther and farther away."*

(hahahaha – ok, bad joke, sorry) Next -

## <u>Should I Tell Anyone I Got A Deer?</u>
MOST DEFINITELY! **It is a requirement**
that after you get your deer loaded up
into your vehicle, that you report your
kill to what is known as a "check-in
station" within so many hours of the kill
(check your own State for regulations
on this timeframe). **You must take the
deer with you and you must have it
properly tagged when you present
the deer to the check-in station**. They
will record the information of the kill for
data-analysis, giving it to State Game and
Wildlife Management officials. Afterward,
they will affix a metal tag to the deer
showing that you complied with the State
law of reporting to the station within the
proper guidelines.

## <u>What Do I Do With The Deer Now?</u>
After the check-in station attendant has
affixed the metal tag to your deer, you
have a few options to choose from. **You
can take the deer home; you can take
the deer to a processor; you can take
the deer to a taxidermist; or you can
take the deer to a food donation site**.

All of these are up to you – the deer is yours to do what you want with as of now.

1) <u>TAKING THE DEER HOME</u>: If you take the deer home for processing on your own, I suggest that you familiarize yourself beforehand on the correct and proper method in which to process and preserve your own deer meat. If you are a beginner, maybe have an experienced person help you with the processing this time and then tackle it on your own later.

2) <u>TAKING THE DEER TO A PROCESSOR</u>: This is the most common choice among hunters. You may take your deer to a professional meat processor to process the deer for you. Depending on what you have killed, you can generally count on getting about 50 pounds of meat processed and wrapped for less than $100.00, but check your local processors to secure pricing first. Also, you MUST have the metal tag affixed to the deer for the processor – don't go to the taxidermist first if you plan on going to the processor also – PROCESSOR 1st – TAXIDERMIST 2nd.

3) <u>TAKING THE DEER TO A TAXIDERMIST</u>: If you are going to take the deer to a taxidermist to have the head mounted, be sure that you have done your homework on who is good and who isn't. Being

a licensed taxidermist myself, I have witnessed some of the most horrific mounts ever seen (*not my own*) in this industry. There are many nightmarish stories out there about bad taxidermists so take heed to these warnings. The last thing you want to do is turn your beautiful deer you worked hard for over to some half-wit that has no idea what he is doing.

4) <u>TAKING THE DEER TO DONATE</u>:
Many States have sites that are set up to collect deer for families in need of food. If you have a deer that you don't especially want, this is a great way to help others in need and will give you an '*attaboy*' too.

# Chapter Five

# AFTER THE SEASON

## FAST FACT
**One of the most important things you can do after the season is to take care of your equipment. This means place it in air-tight bags and store it in a dry, safe place until you are ready to use it for the next hunting season.**

## What Do I Do With All My Stuff?
The first thing I do myself is I take a personal inventory of everything I used and what was needed and what wasn't. I  also note what worked and what didn't. This helps me prepare for the next season using the right equipment that worked best for the need. Next, after washing all of my clothing in 'scent free' laundry detergents, **I personally put everything I "wear" into scent-lock bags with a charcoal pad to help absorb any odors that may leak into the bag in-between seasons**. As far as my equipment goes, if it isn't something I need to practice with in the off-season (notice I said you can practice in the off-season too?), I put it in a LARGE duffle bag with charcoal pads in it also. Believe me, you can not imagine the scents that will attack your clothing

and your equipment in the off-season, and by taking extra precautions now, you will have better success later. Your larger items like your stands and your cases, etc. can be put into a closet or a room where you can control what goes in and what doesn't. I have a "gear room" just for my hunting gear and NOTHING goes in there unless I say it does.

## **What Can I Do To Get Better At This?**
This is an extremely easy question to answer. If you read very, very carefully, I think you just may become a better hunter for your efforts. Ok, ready? Here it is:

| STUDY | **PRACTICE** | SCOUT |
|---|---|---|
| **PRACTICE** | STUDY | **PRACTICE** |
| SCOUT | **PRACTICE** | STUDY |
| **PRACTICE** | SCOUT | **PRACTICE** |

## **AND THEN PRACTICE AGAIN!**

If you aren't ready in your own back yard, you will never be ready in the field when it really counts. **Study** all the information you can get your hands on about deer hunting; **Practice** in all types of shooting positions and scenarios; **Scout** any areas that you think you might be hunting next year, and then scout them again.

I know I keep harping about practice, but if you ever talk to a deer hunter, there is a little thing called "buck fever" they will tell you about that will lock you up bigger'n an oversized chunk of cheese! You will be ready, or so you think, until that big brute walks right out in front of you. Once you see him you will start shaking like you did when your daddy realized that you used his brand new Sears & Roebuck variable-speed drill as a pistol and left it outside to rust (did "I" do that?). It ain't fun!

So to add this factor on top of an inexperienced hunter who hasn't practiced enough, you might as well just shoot straight up in the air and hope that the slug or the arrow you just fired finds its mark on the way down. Your chances will be just about the same. Practice – and then practice again. PLEEEEAAAASSSSE?!

# SCOUTING TIPS

**picture of a low-cover deer trail**

When you are scouting in the woods, you should pay particular attention to certain 'trails' that deer use. These trails are left from heavy usage back and forth from bedding areas and feeding areas. Does typically walk on top of ridges, and bucks typically follow at a lower level along a hillside so as not to be seen by both sides of the hill (they don't want to be 'skylined' either). The trail in the previous picture is on the downside of the ridge so it is very possible that it could be that of the bucks following their "ladies" through the woods.

**picture of a deer's hoof print**

A deer's hoof print is very recognizable. It looks like two elongated tear drops and if it is a buck of any size, you will also see two 'holes' about 1"-2" apart at the back side of the print. This print is pointing in the direction of the deer's travel (right) and looks to be that of a large doe. A very good sign if you are hunting for meat.

Many times it is advantageous to 'age' the deer in which you are tracking through the woods in order to ascertain whether or not it is a mature deer or a yearling that you are following. Remember, you are after either a large doe (for meat) or a large buck (for trophy and meat). **Killing smaller deer only creates a herd of small deer – so let them grow up** – there will be plenty more trophy bucks out there if you only take larger deer. Let young ones walk and eventually all you will be shooting at are big mature deer as nature and time takes their courses.

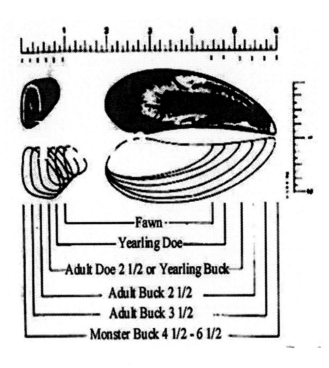

Fawn
Yearling Doe
Adult Doe 2 1/2 or Yearling Buck
Adult Buck 2 1/2
Adult Buck 3 1/2
Monster Buck 4 1/2 - 6 1/2

The previous guide can help you identify the deer that you are tracking thus eliminate timely mistakes of tracking a deer that is too young to harvest. Learn this guide – it will make you a better hunter in the long run and assist you in narrowing your search for the deer you are wanting to harvest.

**picture of a deer's feces ('poop')**

Another great sign is that of the deer's droppings. These droppings look like small rabbit pellets or beans. Many times an experienced hunter can dissect the deer's droppings and determine what and when it ate last. This will help greatly in locating food plots for future set-ups. If you can identify what a deer is eating, then you can usually find where it is eating at. And of course, if you can find where it is eating at, you can usually locate its trails to the food plot from the bedding areas, and like we've said all along, this is where you want to set-up.

**author showing a deer's rub
on a small sapling tree**

This is one of the flags that you will see in the woods that will excite you to the point of doing the "*Snoopy dance.*" It is called a "rub" and a rub is a tell-tale sign that a buck is in the area. Remember that a buck rubs these trees down in order to remove the velvety material from their racks (antlers) as well as mark a perimeter of his territory. It's a GOOD SIGN to find.

**close-up picture of same rub**

If you can find 8-10 rubs within a few hundred yards, you have identified what is commonly known to deer hunters as a 'rub line'. It would be in your best interest to note where this perimeter is and set-up down-range (down-wind) of this area for best results.

**author inspecting a large scrape he has found**

At last, the all time best deer sign you could ever find in the woods (without seeing the big brute himself). The 'scrape' is the sign that shows a buck is not only marking his territory for travel purposes, but he is marking it as an invitation to all the doe in the area that he is the one they want to be mating with...in this area.

**author kneeling at the same scrape he found**

The scrape will ultimately tell you, the hunter, just when the last time the buck passed by and 'freshened it up' for his future female counterparts to define as well. A scrape that has been visited often will be *moist* in the very center where the buck has urinated, leaving his mark and his identity. It is a sign that tells much about the deer you are hunting and you want to spend a lot of time investigating it without touching it in any way, shape, or form.

A scrape is started by the buck scraping the debris back from under a low-lying limb. He does this to clear a spot down to the earth so he can identify himself within the scrape itself. Next, he straddles the scrape and urinates in the middle of it creating a moist "odor-identifier" for does to recognize. Once he is done urinating in the middle of the scrape, he then takes his front hoof and steps right in the middle of the urine-saturated earth and puts his weight down on it forcing his hoof print into the 'muddy earth' showing his "size" to the interested doe. While standing in the middle of the scrape, the buck then begins to thrash the limb above with his antlers (rack) attempting to break it as high as possible for two reasons: 1) to spread his scent over the limbs as an additional odor-identifier, and 2) to show the interested doe that he is 'big and tall' as well. It is all a ritual to show any interested doe that this buck is big, tall, and powerful so they will choose him to mate with. He be "*HE-BUCK*" (He-Man).

Well, there you have it. I guess that just about wraps up this edition of **Deer Hunting 101** other than the Glossary of Terms and the Venison Recipes I have included at the end of this book.

I'm glad you took the time to review my material and I hope that you will take to heart some of the things I have mentioned in this book. If you do, I guarantee that you will definitely increase your chances of not only seeing more deer on your next hunt, but actually taking one down *and finding it*. This is the reward you are after.

Be sure to check out my other books coming out. You can watch for these at **www.booksbydave.com**. I would also like to ask that you drop me an email from my website after you finish this book just so I know who has read it and who will be taking the knowledge from here into the field with them. If you get a trophy buck, of course, send me a pic so I can share in your excitement too!

But for now, take care of yourself; stay safe; and remember to always pass your knowledge on to those that need it. There are plenty of deer out there for all of us.

Goodbye, Good Hunting, and God Bless!

# GLOSSARY OF TERMS

## A

**Abomasum**  The abomasum is the fourth chamber of a deer's stomach. This chamber, along with the omasum (which is the third chamber), is considered the true stomach. These chambers help further the digestive process by producing acids which break down the food particles and the microorganisms from animals that have stomachs consisting of four chambers.

**Adapt**  A term used describing how animals change to coexist with their surroundings during a specific time period.

**Aggregation**  Deer that are forced to group together due to the low amounts of food available.

**Antler**  An antler is a growth on top of the head formed of bone, starting at eleven months of age. They are ornamental structures prized by hunters. They are also prized by the deer themselves in the sense that they are used for gaining dominance and attracting mates. Antlers are unique to mammals and are the only type of appendage to grow, fall off and start growing again yearly. The size of the antlers depends on the nutrition in the diet.

## B

**Bachelor Group**  Bucks congregate in groups separate from everyone else during spring and summer.

**Bawl**  An intense sound made by a traumatized deer, used as an alarm.

**Beam**  Main branches of antlers from which the forks grow.

**Bedding Area**  Trampled areas where deer rest. The spots are picked for their concealment and views of approaching deer. Deer usually have a few beds within their home range.

**Bleat**  A type of vocalization deer make.

**Bolus**  Mass of food that is rechewed, becoming cud.

**Boone & Crockett Club**  A system of scoring animals harvested by rifle hunters.

**Break Line**  A line of demarcation between the old timber and the new growth. Deer "hold" to these break lines and use them as new scraping and rubbing areas. They use the break lines both in a parallel and perpendicular manner.

**Browsing**  The way a deer eats. They eat quickly, chewing just enough to swallow. This limits their exposure to predators.

**Brow Tine**  The first fork of the antler on a deer.

**Buck**  A buck is a male deer. The male is discernible from the females by the set of antlers atop its head for seven months. Otherwise males and females are similar looking.

**Buck Rub**  A male deer lowers his head to scrape his antlers against a tree. He does this for two reasons: To help polish and clean away velvet, and to instinctively get ready for competition of the breeding season. The chosen tree usually is less than 4 inches in diameter.

# C

**Calling**  Imitating the different sounds deer make to lure them into shooting range.

**Camouflage**  Coloration that helps the body blend in with the surrounding environments- whether it's a fawn with spots or a hunter's clothing.

**Carnivore**  Carnivores are predators that almost exclusively live off the flesh of other animals.

**Character Point**  The first point extending from the main beam upwards on whitetail's antlers.

**Conditioning**  A way of learning from experiences. Bucks become conditioned to be active only at nighttime during hunting season. They learn that there is little pressure during darkness than there is in daylight.

**Coniferous Trees**  Trees which bear cones. These trees do not lose their leaves in the fall, which makes them a great food source for deer in the winter. A good example of a coniferous tree is the pine tree.

**Cover Scents**  A scent used to cover up the human scent during hunting.

**Cud**  Cud is food that goes through several steps to be regurgitated to be chewed more, and fully digested to finalize the process. Food that is fibrous requires this process to be repeated again. Food that is less fibrous and easily digestible may go through only one rotation of steps.

# D

**Deadfall**  Branches and ground litter that serves as concealment when the hunter is on the ground.

**Deciduous Trees**  Trees which lose their leaves every winter, only to have them grow back in the spring. These trees are found throughout the US, with high concentrations in the forests of the Northeast.

**Deer Yard**  Small areas where large numbers of deer congregate during the winter. These areas are popular either for the shelter or warmth they provide, or for their abundance in food. Deer yards cause tension and aggression among deer due to the crowding and the fights over food.

**Dispersal**  When fawns leave their mothers to establish their own home range.

**DNR**  Department of Natural Resources.

**Doe**  A doe is a female deer.

**Dominant Buck**  Dominant bucks compete and fight their way up the ranks of a group of bucks. This social hierarchy is followed by the other deer in the group by being submissive.

**Dominant Floater**  Dominant floaters are older, large bucks that travel through different ranges while still maintaining their ranking. They associate with many groups of deer, but do not form close associations.

**Drop Tine**  An antler point that drops straight down off the main beam of the antlers of whitetail males.

# E

**Estrus**  A two to four day period when doe are capable of breeding. It is only during this time that a doe will allow a buck to approach her.

# F

**Fawn**  A fawn is a baby deer, distinguished from adults by a white spotted coat. Newborn fawns are almost scentless, saving them from being noticed by predators. Fawns instinctively play by quickly running away from their mother and back again, sometimes bucking and zigzagging. This gives them practice for eluding predators.

**Flehmen**  Also known as a lip curl. A buck will curl his lips and suck scents into his vomeronasal gland in order to analyze them.

**Forage**  Another word for the food that deer eat.

**Forehead Gland**  The gland in the forehead of the deer they used to leave scent on branches and twigs.

# G

**Gallop**  The high speed running of whitetail deer trying to escape dangerous predators.

**Gestation**  The length of time for pregnancy which varies from species to species.

**Groom**  A doe and her fawn licking each other to establish a bonding relationship.

**Grunt**  A type of vocalization used by deer (mainly the male deer referred to as 'bucks').

# H

**Habitat**  The type of environment that supports wildlife such as deer and all of its activities.

**Herbivore**  Animals that exclusively live on vegetation.

**Hierarchy** A system within groups of animals that has a defined ranking system and places each individual animal in a pecking order, with one dominant animal being at the top and the rest at the bottom of the order.

**Home Range** The area in which a deer lives in throughout its life which contains all of its necessities such as food, shelter, etc.

**Horns** Not to be confused with deer antlers that are shed each year, horns are permanent and never shed.

# I

**Imprint** When a fawn or mother deer (doe) realize who the other is and only responds to each other.

**Instinct** Behavior that is naturally ingrained into the animal in question.

**Interdigital Gland** A gland on a deer located between the toes that serves to leave scent as it walks.

# L

**Lick** The area that a deer licks (ie: branches, leaves, etc.) during the breeding season used as a method of communicating to other deer.

# M

**Metatarsal Gland** A gland located halfway between the toes and the heel of the foot on the outside of the hind leg.

# N

**Nasal Gland** The gland in deer located inside the nostrils that is primarily used for lubrication purposes.

**Nocturnal** Nocturnal means activity during nighttime hours. The reason why deer can move around in the dark is because they see well at night. There is a membrane at the back of the eye that specially filters light, allowing them keen vision in low light conditions.

**Non-Typical**  Antlers that have points growing off the back of the main beam or off of other points.

**NRA**  National Rifle Association – an organization in support of the use of firearms. (good organization!)

# O

**Odocileus**  The genus of North American deer that includes whitetail, blacktail, and mule deer.

**Odocoileus Virginianus**  The scientific name given for the whitetail deer.

**Omasum**  The third chamber of the deer's stomach which along with the abomasum, is considered to be the true stomach of the deer. This chamber's main function in the digestive process is to absorb water from the food mass which is being passed through the system.

**Omnivore**  Animals that eat both vegetation and flesh.

# P

**Paunch**  Another word for a filled stomach. The deer has a paunch after it has quickly eaten several pounds of food where it will then retire to rest and digest the substance by regurgitating it and rechewing its cud before swallowing it again.

**Pedicle**  A bony growth that protrudes from the head of male deer (bucks) that are the beginnings of antler growth. Although antlers are shed annually, pedicles remain on the buck throughout its entire life.

**Pheromone**  Scented chemicals given off from deer that serve as communication methods to other deer.

**Photoperiod**  Based on the amount of light during the day, it is at this time that the deer begin producing hormones to prepare for the breeding season.

**Piloerection**  The process by which keeps a deer

warm in the wintry months. The deer will contract tiny muscles all over its skin which raises the hair on its body. These raised hairs trap air pockets which provide a layer of insulation for the deer when it is extremely cold.

**Pituitary**  The main hormone producing gland of the deer's body which also controls antler growth and acts as a stimulant for the onset of estrus, etc.

**Poaching**  The killing of animals illegally, whether it is during the season or not, and whether the animals are endangered species or not.

**Pope and Young**  A scoring system for those animals that are killed by bow and arrow.

**Population Density**  The number of deer in certain areas.

**Portable Stand**  A tree stand that is smaller in size and usually strapped to a tree in a temporary manner so that a hunter may carry it in with him and remove it as he leaves the area. Some States only allow portable stands on State property.

**Pre-orbital Gland**  The gland located near the front of the deer's eye (also known as the tear duct) which is used to rub scent on branches and leaves for communicative purposes.

**Pre-rut**  The time period which occurs prior to the actual rutting period (mating period) when deer are preparing to breed. Deer become easily agitated and overly aggressive during this time and bucks (male deer) undergo many changes including the shedding of the velvety material on their racks, as well as engaging in semi-competitive sparring matches to establish male dominance within the herd.

**Predators**  Any animal which feeds off of other animals in order to live. Common predators of the whitetail deer include, but are not limited to: Coyotes, Wolves, and Mountain Lions (Cougars).

# R

**Rack**  A set of antlers on a deer.

**Rattling**  The method of recreating the noise of two male deer fighting by banging or clashing together two sets of antlers or utilizing a 'rattlin' bag'. Used to lure deer into shooting range of your location.

**Refuge**  A place where animals have plentiful food and supportive environmental materials.

**Reticulum**  The second chamber of the deer's stomach used to break down plant materials and store already chewed cud into clumps for digestive and purging purposes.

**Rub-off**  The process a male deer (buck) goes through to remove the velvety material from its antlers during the pre-rut stage. The buck will use a tree or bush, or any protruding object (ie: fence post, etc.) to remove the substance from its rack.

**Rubs**  Bucks (male deer) rub trees and tree branches with their antlers displaying dominance and marking their territory for breeding purposes.

**Rumen**  The first chamber of the four-part stomach of the deer. It is mainly used as a digestive chamber containing billions of micro-organisms designed to break down food into materials useable in the digestive track.

**Ruminants**  Animals with four-chambered stomachs. These four chambers are called" Rumen, Reticulum, Omasum, and Abomasum. All four chambers are needed to process the large amount of food eaten by the deer.

**Rump Patch**  The area on a deer around its tail, rump, and upper legs that is white in color.

**Rut**  The time period that lasts around 4-6 months that makes up the breeding season of the deer. Hormones in the pituitary gland in the deer's brain trigger instinctive behaviors which in turn tell the deer there is a need to breed. Bucks (male deer) become aggressive with each other to compete for does (female deer) and thus get into fights by clashing their racks together in hopes of downing and gorging their opponent to either flee or die in the process.

# S

**Scavengers**  Animals which feed off of other animals for sustenance (life). Scavengers are different from predators because they only feed off of the dead carcass of animals they discover – not animals they have hunted and killed themselves.

**Scouting**  The time spent in the woods (all year long) locating and charting deer activities to familiarize one's self as to how the deer act and what they do in all seasons. This information gathered is vital to the hunter if he wants to take a deer during his hunting season.

**Scrapes**  When a buck (male deer) paws at the ground making a bare mark and then urinates in the middle of it, letting does (female deer) in the area know that he wants to breed.

**Sebaceous Gland**  One of the building blocks of all of the glands – releases lipids which are used to carry scents and this is how the deer communicate.

**Shining**  The act of shining a light at a deer in the darkness making its eyes seem as if they are glowing. Many poachers use this method to kill deer illegally as they can sit at an open field and shine a light – once they see the eyes glowing, they shoot between the eyes. Remember, THIS IS ILLEGAL – DON'T TRY IT! NEVER!

**Signposting**  The same as a 'rub' where antlers are rubbed against trees, tree branches, fence posts, etc. in order to assist in the cleaning away of the velvety material that is attached to a buck's antlers. It is also a sign to other deer that the buck (male deer) is ready for competing for the breeding season.

**Snort**  The sound made by a deer when air is forced through the nostrils and the result is a loud, airy noise.

**Sparring**  The method by which male deer (bucks) establish their dominance within the herd. Sparring usually occurs during the pre-rut when bucks' antlers are hard and strong. When sparring, two bucks will approach each other with their head low, and then lock antlers. They then push each other until one runs off succumbing to the other. Sparring is also used for bucks to estimate the size and strength of their antlers so when it comes time to use them, they will have an idea of what their limits are.

**Specifist**  Deer have narrow snouts which allows them to be picky eaters since they feed on vegetation.

**Stampede**  The awesome sight of an entire herd of deer running in the same direction at the same time.

**Stand Hunting**  Erecting a stand high enough off of the ground so as to be out of sight, smell, and hearing range of the deer's head height. Stands are usually erected anywhere from 10'-0 to 30'-0 off of the ground.

**Still Hunting**  This type of hunting is where the hunter moves extremely slow through the woods in hopes of sneaking up on a sleeping deer.

**Strap-on Stand**  A portable stand large enough to hold a hunter yet small enough to be able to strap it to a tree trunk high in the air.

**Sudoriferous**  One of two glands which is the building block of all of the other glands (the other is the sebaceous gland). This gland is a tubular sweat gland located just below the deer's skin (hide). The gland is responsible for most of the chemical processing that allows the communicative methods of the deer to work.

# T

**Tail Flag**  The all-too-familiar sign we see in the woods as hunters. This method is used to warn other deer of danger. Upon sensing a possible dangerous situation, the deer will RAISE ITS TAIL HALFWAY. If the danger is then confirmed, the deer will finish raising its tail to full height and flee from the area it perceives as being dangerous. The tail flag not only provides a visual warning sign to other deer, but also provides a flag for which the younger deer can follow mom as she flees from the dangerous area in order to escape rapidly.

**Tapetum**  A membrane on the back of the deer's eye which reflects light, thus, improving the deer's vision.

**Tarsal Gland**  The gland in deer located on the inside of the hind leg. The deer urinates on the gland which then mixes with oils produced from the gland. This gland is said to be used to excrete a 'danger signal' by slapping the two glands together bursting them and sending a rancid scent into the air warning other deer to stay out of the area.

**Taxidermist**  A person who preserves wildlife through a unique artistry for display purposes (the author of this book is a State & Federally licensed taxidermist also).

**Tend**  A buck (male deer) will stay close by a female deer (doe) which is in heat, not aggressively, but waiting for the doe to show him a sign that she is ready for breeding. This is said to be 'tending his doe'.

**Thicket**  A dense area of coverage that whitetail deer like to hide in so as not to be discovered by predators.

**Topographical Map**  An overhead trajectory of a specific area that shows the lay of the land in both elevations and depressions. Very helpful in locating areas that may harbor deer if you are not familiar to that area.

**Trophy**  Typically a mature buck (male deer) with a large set of antlers that will ultimately be used for mounting purposes by a Taxidermist. However, some hunters consider their first deer, or even every deer to be a trophy to them, regardless of sex or size.

**Typical**  Antlers that only have points growing off of the front side of the main beam.

# V

**Velvet**  The protective covering encasing the growing antler on a male deer (buck). It is a layer of very soft skin that nourishes the growing bone by supplying blood to it, but once it begins to dry out, the buck rubs it against a tree or branch to rub it off because it 'itches'.

**Venison**  The meat of a deer.

**Vomolfaction**  The sixth sense of a deer. In addition to the five senses that are common to most mammals, it is a process by which a buck sucks a doe's urine and then discards it. This helps the buck determine if the doe is approaching breeding season or not.

# VENISON (Deer) RECIPES
## *(just for starters)*

The secret to great venison is to not cook it over high heat and _be sure not to overcook it_.

Venison is much drier than beef and needs to be sautéed in a little butter or margarine before cooking. If you like your beef 'well-done' then chances are you will not like venison because 'well done' venison is like shoe leather. But, if you like your beef medium to medium-rare, you will absolutely love the flavor that venison brings to your dinner table!

## Grilled Venison Steaks
Venison Steaks (6-8)

1/2 – 3/4 cup Heinz 57 Sauce
1/4 – 1/2 cup straight honey
garlic salt, black pepper

Season venison steaks with garlic salt and black pepper (to taste). Mix Heinz 57 sauce with honey. Spread over both sides of steak. Grill (or broil at 425 degrees) for approx. 15 minutes. Turn once and brush with sauce again, cooking for an additional 5-10 minutes (as preferred). Remove and serve hot. Enjoy!

## Venison Roast
(Use either sirloin tip or rump round)

The best way to a tender, juicy roast is to bake only to the point of being medium to medium-rare. More than this could cause the roast to dry out and become tough. To check this, you can use a meat thermometer:

Rare = 130-135 degrees

Medium-Rare = 135-140 degrees

Medium = 140-145 degrees

First, brown the roast on all sides in a little hot oil. Season the roast with a combination of celery salt, coarse ground pepper, and garlic powder (I like a little spicy pepper also).

Place the roast on oven rack in a baking pan. Lay several thin strips of bacon over the top. Roast at 425 degrees for about 15 minutes per pound of meat.

Remove, pour juices over top of roast and serve. Enjoy!

## Venison Stroganoff

1-1/2 pounds venison steak, cut in ¼" strips
3 tablespoons flour
1/2 teaspoon salt
1/4 teaspoon pepper
3 tablespoons butter or margarine
2 cups sliced mushrooms (thick)
1 large sliced onion
1/4 cup flour
2 cups beef broth
1/8 cup tomato paste
2 cups sour cream
noodles, cooked (qty. per family size)

Mix 3 tablespoons flour, salt and pepper; add venison strips and roll to coat. Melt butter in a large skillet. Add venison and cook over medium-high heat until browned. Remove meat and add mushrooms and onions. Stir in remaining flour. Add broth and tomato paste and stir. Return the venison to the skillet and simmer gently for about 10 minutes until heated through. Add the sour cream and stir until well mixed. Serve the stroganoff over hot cooked noodles. Enjoy!

## Venison Chili

1 pound dry kidney beans
1-1/2 pounds ground venison
1 pound venison stew meat (1/2-inch chunks)
2 tablespoons oil
2 cloves garlic, minced
3 teaspoons chili powder
1 teaspoon salt
1/2 teaspoon pepper
28-ounce can tomatoes, diced
1 large onion, diced
1 green pepper, diced
1 large green chili pepper, diced
1/4 teaspoon cumin
2 tablespoons parsley, chopped
1/4 cup all purpose flour

Rinse beans and place in a large soup pan. Add 2 quarts hot water and 2 teaspoons salt; cover the pot and bring to a boil. Boil gently for about 2 hours, until beans are tender. Brown meat in a large skillet containing oil and garlic. Add chili powder, salt and pepper. Cover and sauté for an hour. Drain the beans and add 1-1/2 quarts hot water, tomatoes, onion, peppers, cumin and parsley. Simmer for an hour, and then add meat mixture. Stir flour into 1/2 cup water to form a paste and blend into chili to thicken. Simmer for about half an hour, season to taste and serve. Enjoy!

## Venison Gravy on Biscuits

1-1/2 pound ground venison
1 can sliced mushrooms (4-ounce)
1 can cream of mushroom soup
1 can milk
salt and pepper to taste

Brown the venison in a large fry pan. Add mushrooms and cook for a 3-4 minutes. Add mushroom soup and milk. Stir and cook until smooth and hot. Salt and pepper to taste and serve over hot biscuits. Enjoy!

## Venison Shish Kabobs

2 lb. venison (cut into 2" chunks)
Italian Dressing
1 can pineapple chunks
12 cherry tomatoes
1 large onion (cut up into 1-1/2" chunks)
1 green pepper (cut up into 1-1/2" chunks)
I lb. whole mushrooms

Marinate venison chunks overnight in Italian dressing. Put meat and remaining ingredients onto skewers in random order.

Grill over open flame, brushing with Italian dressing for 15-20 min. turning often until done to your preference. Serve and enjoy!

## Dave's Venison Stew

2 pounds venison (cut into 1-1/2" chunks)
2 cans Campbell's cream of mushroom soup
1 env. dry Lipton's onion-mushroom soup mix
6 skinned & cubed potatoes
1 cup of hot water

Soak venison in several rinses of fresh water. Drain venison and place in crock-pot. Add cubed potatoes and cover with cream of mushroom soup. Sprinkle dry onion-mushroom soup mix on top and add cup of hot water. Cook on low or medium setting overnight (approximately eight hours) and stir several times while cooking (yup, get up). Venison should fall apart when done. Make enough for the next day because this stew is even better when reheated. Enjoy!

## Dave's Deer Jerky *(my personal favorite)*

Slice 5 lbs deer meat into 1/4" thick slices
Mix the following ingredients in a large bowl:
1/2 bottle of liquid smoke (2 oz) - *optional*
1 cup of Worcestershire sauce
1 cup of soy sauce
1 teaspoon of seasoning salt
2 teaspoons of garlic powder
1 teaspoon of onion powder
1 teaspoon of pepper *(cayan pepper optional)*
1/2 bottle of Tabasco sauce (or more to taste)

Marinate meat in bowl overnight (soaked)

Either lay strips of meat in cookie sheet or hang from rack by toothpicks with cookie sheet underneath to catch drippings

Place meat in oven at 125 to 140 degrees for 10 to 12 hours. Cook until meat barely snaps when bent

Keep plenty hid for yourself, and serve. Enjoy!

# HE HUNG THERE FOR ME

As I sit here today hanging from this big tree

I can't help but realize what this means to me.

The weather is perfect, the wind is just right

I'm hoping to see one walk into my sights.

I watch very closely should movement occur

I listen intently for sounds to be heard.

I've practiced real hard to prepare for this day

It's something I do - it's my form of 'play'.

But if I don't get one I'll be glad that I went

This time for reflection will be time well spent.

You see this tree that I'm hanging from

Is a vivid reminder of the death of His Son.

I choose to come out here and hang from this tree

As He hung from one too, for you and for me.

He stretched out His arms
and took nails in His hands

So we would be saved, it was part of His plan.

So hanging for pleasure is not to compare

To the blood that He shed, it just doesn't seem fair.

I guess like a parent, He gave up His life

As I know that I would for my kids or my wife.

So if you're a hunter and sit way up high

Take time to accept Him, you're not to deny.

For now is the time to reflect on His death

Remember His words as He took His last breath.

"Forgive them Father; they know not what they do"

Could you say the same, if you were in His shoes?

Accept Him and love Him and talk to Him now

He listens even when you don't understand how.

His love for you grows each time you seek Him

So open your heart – He'll be your best friend.

He will not care if you've continually failed

Instead He'll remind you of why He was nailed.

So I'll pray for your safety
as you hang from your tree

And hope you reflect on, "He Hung There For Me."

*author: David B. Pruet*

**TO ORDER YOUR COPY OF**

# <u>DEER HUNTING 101</u>
*The Beginner's Guide to Deer Hunting*

(or any other books by this author)

**GO TO THE AUTHOR'S WEBSITE**

## *<u>www.booksbydave.com</u>*